This book belongs to

Unit 1: Showing numbers on abacus

Example 1

The abacus show the number 435
read as four hundred and thirty five

$$400 + 30 + 5 = 435$$

Example 2

The abacus show the number 2315 read as two thousand three hundred and fifteen 2000 + 300 + 10 + 5 = 2315

Exercise 1
Write the value of the abacus

Write the value of the abacus

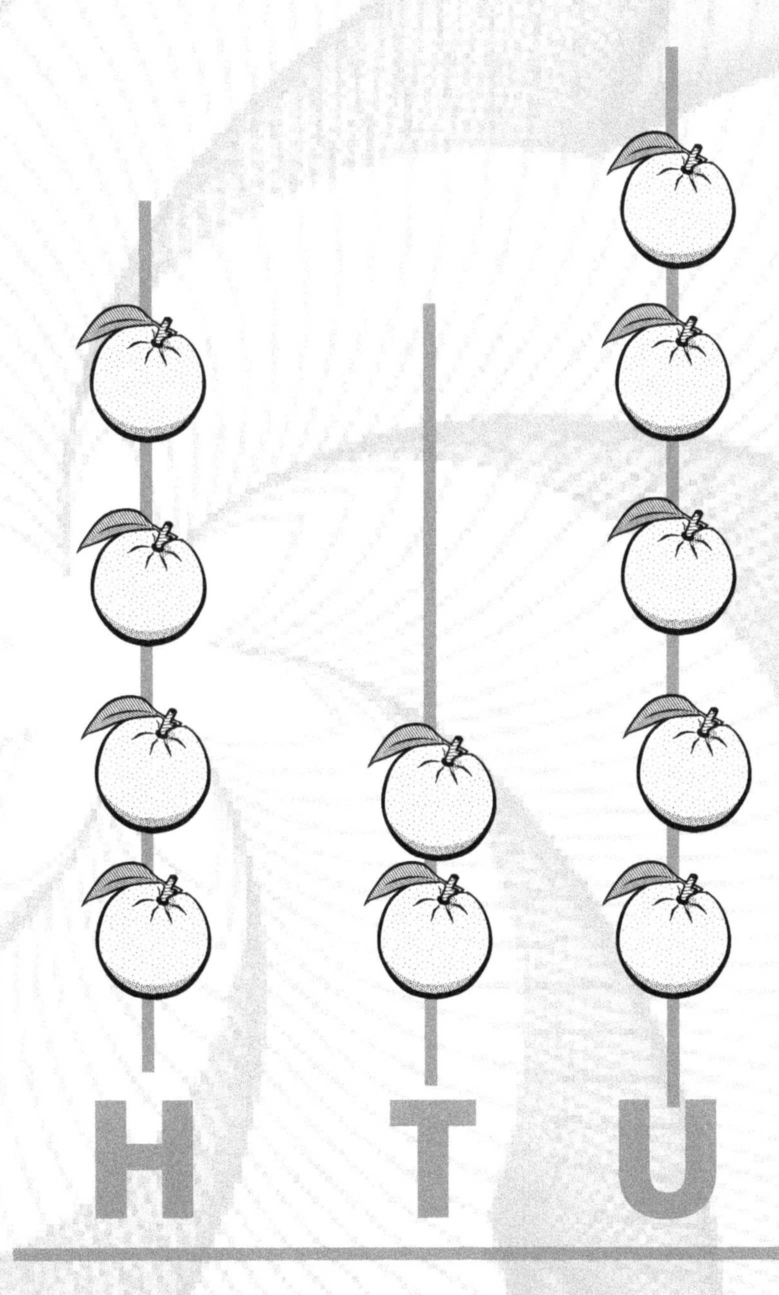

Write the value of the abacus

Write the value of the abacus

Write the value of the abacus

Write the value of the abacus

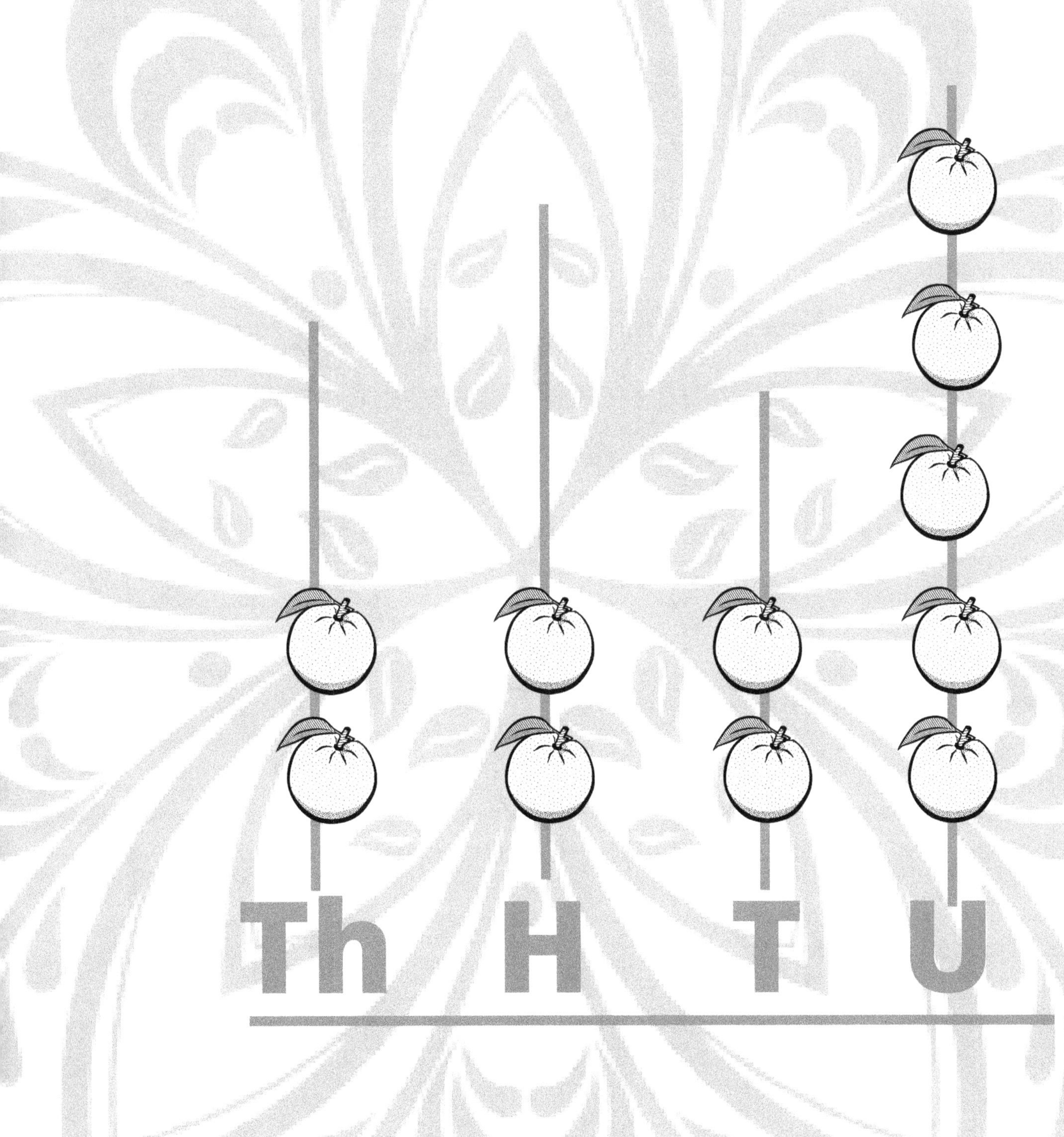

Write the value of the abacus

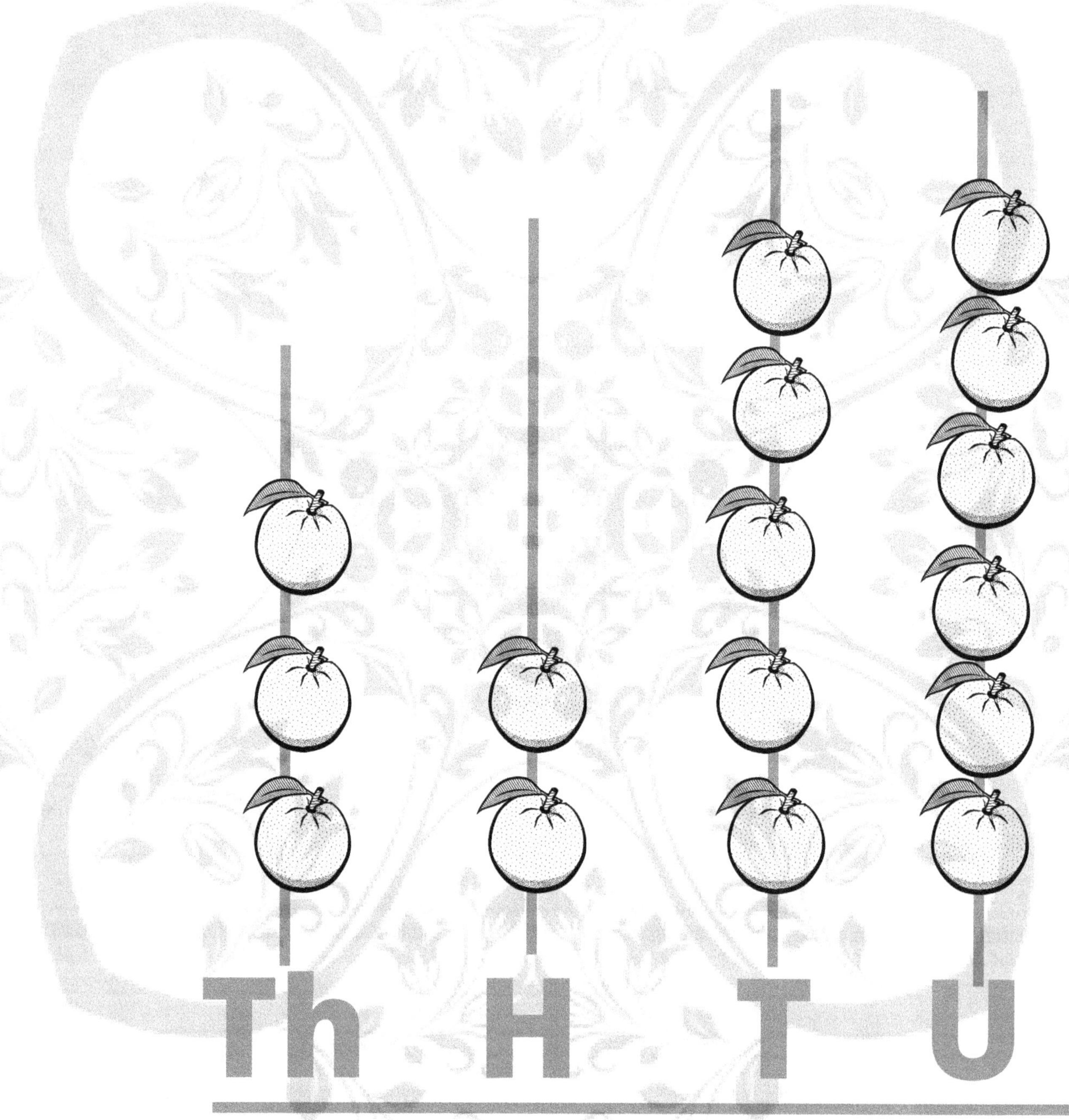

Write the value of the abacus

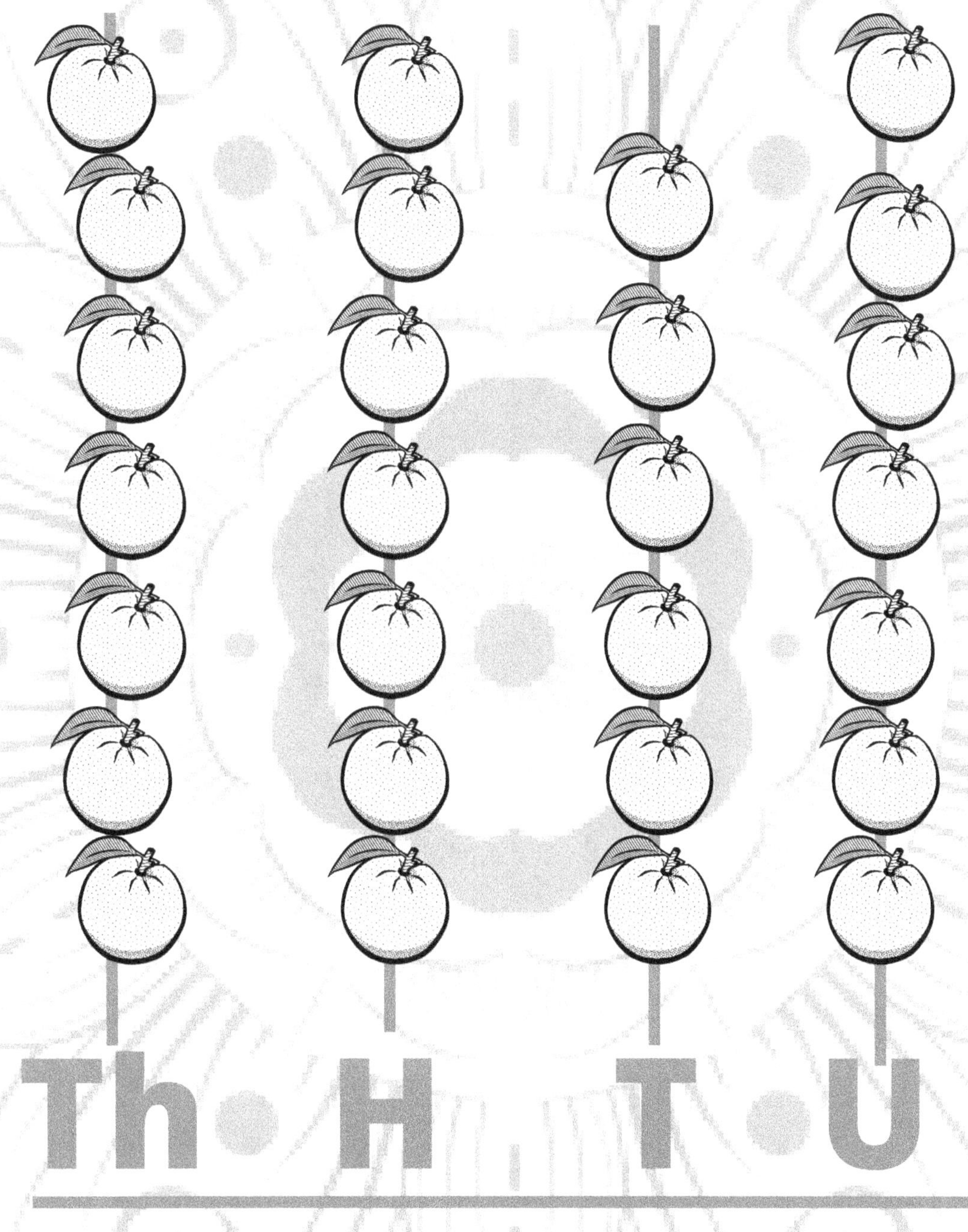

Write the value of the abacus

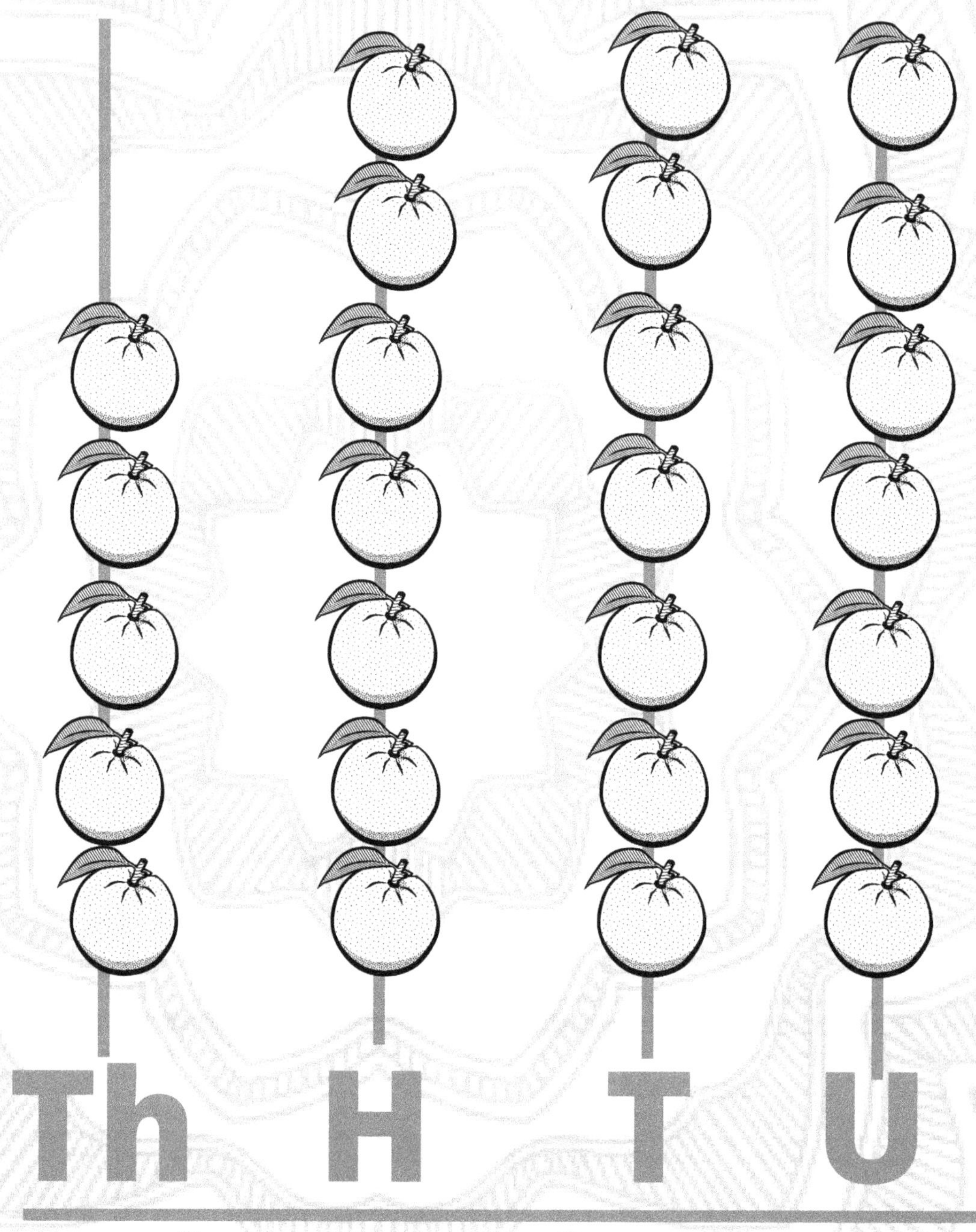

Write the value of the abacus

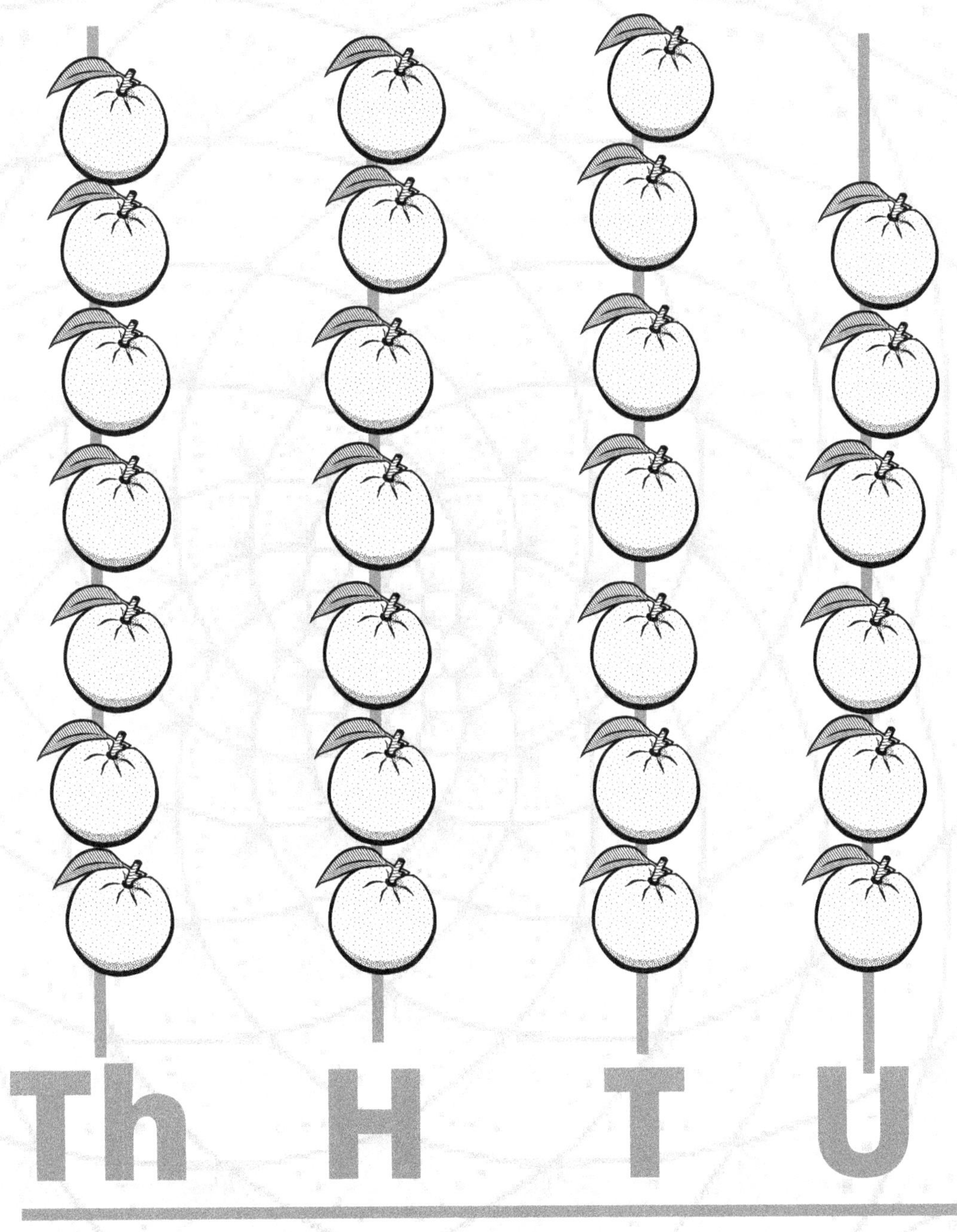

Exercise 2

Write the number shown on the abacus in numeral and word

Write the number shown on the abacus in numeral and word

Write the number shown on the abacus in numeral and word

Write the number shown on the abacus in numeral and word

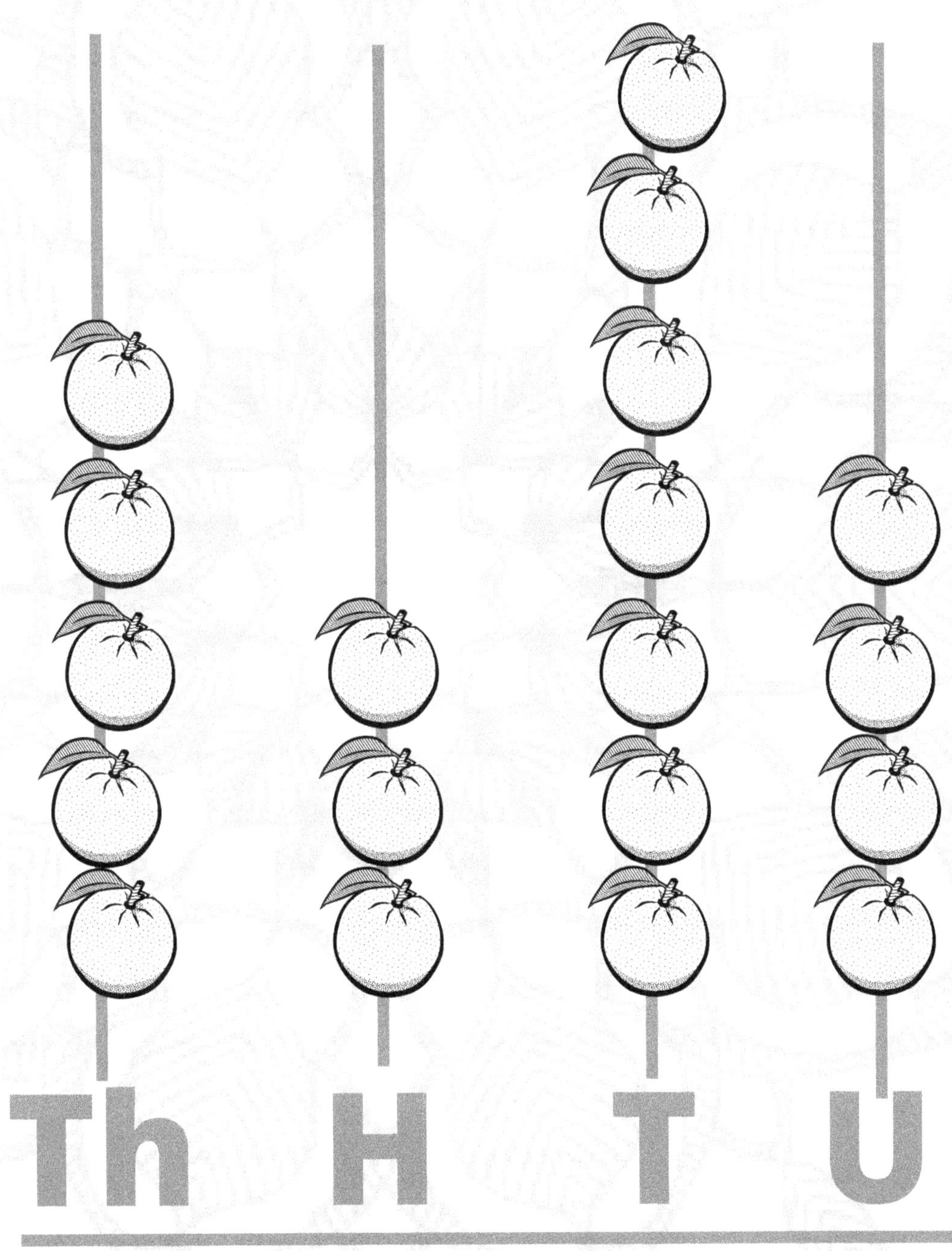

Write the number shown on the abacus in numeral and word

Write the number shown on the abacus in numeral and word

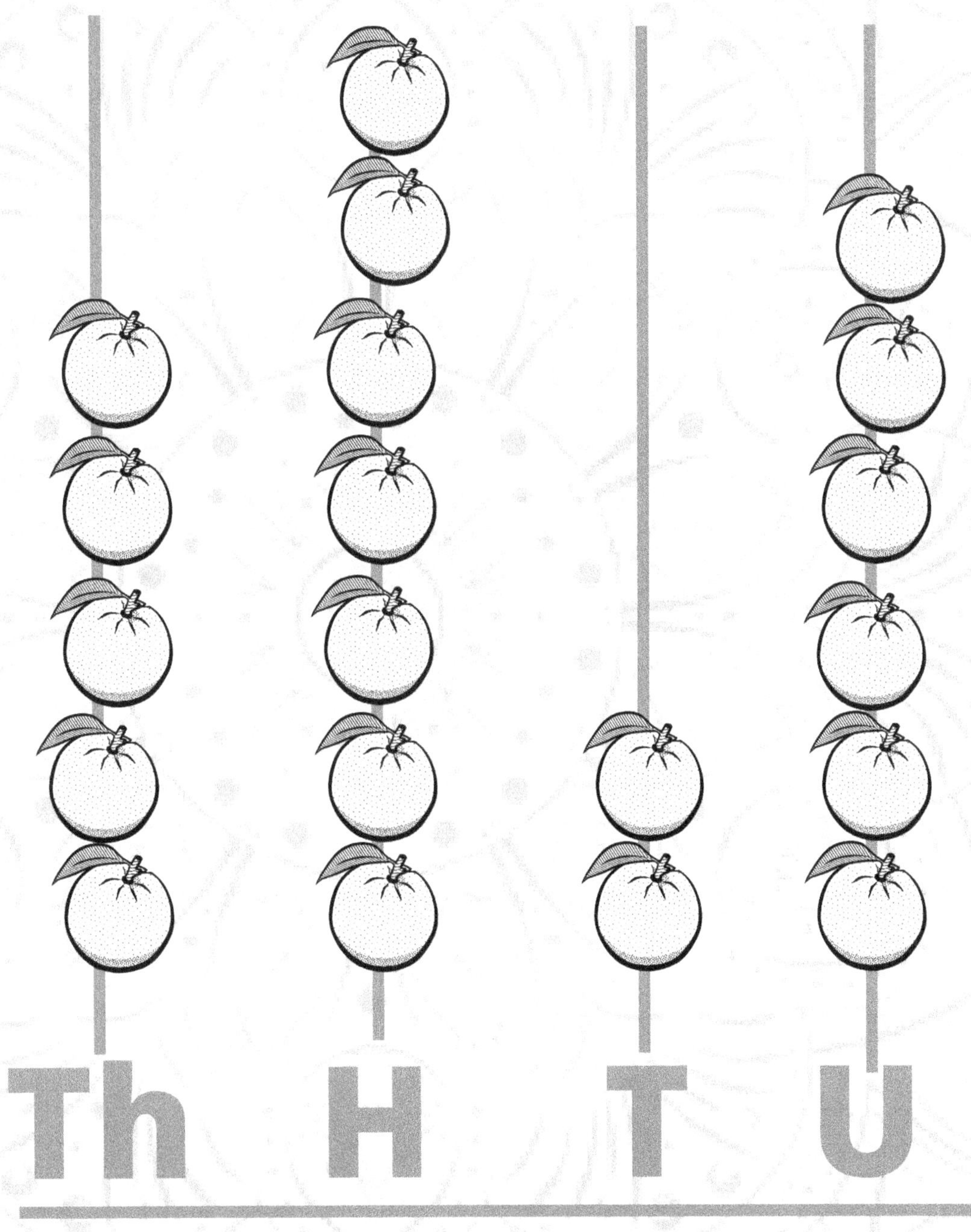

Write the number shown on the
abacus in numeral and word

Exercise 3

Draw an abacus for the
number 321

Draw an abacus for the number 285

Draw an abacus for the number 909

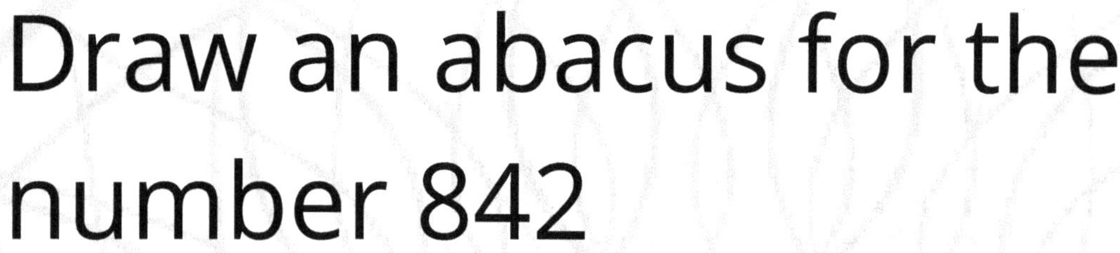

Draw an abacus for the number 5412

Draw an abacus for the number 2906

Draw an abacus for the number 6037

Unit 2: Counting in groups

Count in 4's

	4 in one place 4
	4 in two places 4 + 4 = 8 4 × 2 = 8
	4 in three places 4 + 4 + 4 = 12 4 × 3 = 12
	4 in four places 4 + 4 + 4 + 4 = 16 4 × 4 = 16

200	204	208	212	216	220	224	228	232	236
2050	2054	2058	2062	2064	2068	2072	2076	2082	2086

Exercise 1

Count in 2's copy and complete
each sequence

A. 600, 602, 604, _______, _______, _______,

B. 780, 782, 784, _______, _______, _______,

C. 851, 853, 855, _______, _______, _______,

D. 973, 975, 977, _______, _______, _______,

E. 1001, 1003, 1005, _______, _______, _______,

F. 1001, 1003, 1005, _______, _______, _______,

G. 1065, 1067, 1069, _______, _______, _______,

G. 1109, 1111, 1113, _______, _______, _______,

Count in 4's copy and complete
each sequence

A. 672, 676, 680, _______, _______, _______

B. 777, 781, 785, _______, _______, _______

C. 851, 855, 859, _______, _______, _______

D. 973, 977, 981, _______, _______, _______

E. 1007, 1011, 1015, _______, _______, _______

F. 1034, 1038, 1042, _______, _______, _______

G. 1065, 1069, 1073, _______, _______, _______

G. 1109, 1113, 1117, _______, _______, _______

Count in 6's copy and complete
each sequence

A. 676, 682, 688, _______, _______, _______

B. 777, 783, 789, _______, _______, _______

C. 851, 857, 863, _______, _______, _______

D. 973, 979, 985, _______, _______, _______

E. 1007, 1013, 1019, _______, _______, _______

F. 1034, 1040, 1046, _______, _______, _______

G. 1065, 1071, 1077, _______, _______, _______

G. 1109, 1115, 1121, _______, _______, _______

Count in 8's copy and complete
each sequence

A. 670, 678, 686, ______, ______, ______

B. 772, 780, 788, ______, ______, ______

C. 855, 864, 872, ______, ______, ______

D. 979, 987, 995, ______, ______, ______

E. 1007, 1015, 1023, ______, ______, ______

F. 1036, 1044, 1053, ______, ______, ______

G. 1065, 1073, 1081, ______, ______, ______

G. 1109, 1117, 1125, ______, ______, ______

Exercise 2

There are four books in a bag. How many books are there in:

A. 6 bags

B. 8 bags

C. 10 bags

D. 12 bags

E. 14 bags

F. 18 bags

G. 20 bags

If a box has 8 apples how many apples are there in

A. 6 boxes

B 8 boxes

C. 10 boxes

D. 12 boxes

E. 14 boxes

F.   18 boxes

G.   20 boxes

If a basket contains 12 eggs how many
many eggs are there in

A. 6 baskets

B 8 baskets

C. 10 baskets

D. 12 baskets

E. 14 baskets

F.   18 baskets

G.   20 baskets

How many seconds are there in :

A. 6 minutes

B. 8 minutes

C. 10 minutes

D. 12 minutes

E. 14 minutes

F.   18 minutes

G.   20 minutes

How many days are there in :

A. 2 weeks

B. 4 weeks

C. 10 weeks

D 15 weeks

E. 18 weeks

F.   24 weeks

G.   36 weeks

How many weeks are there in :

A. 2 months

B.   5 months

C. 10 months

D 15 months

E.   18 months

F.   24 months

G.   36 months

How many years are there in :

A. 12 months

B   24 months

C. 36 months

D. 48 months

E. 144 months

F. 720 months

G. 3600 months

Example 1

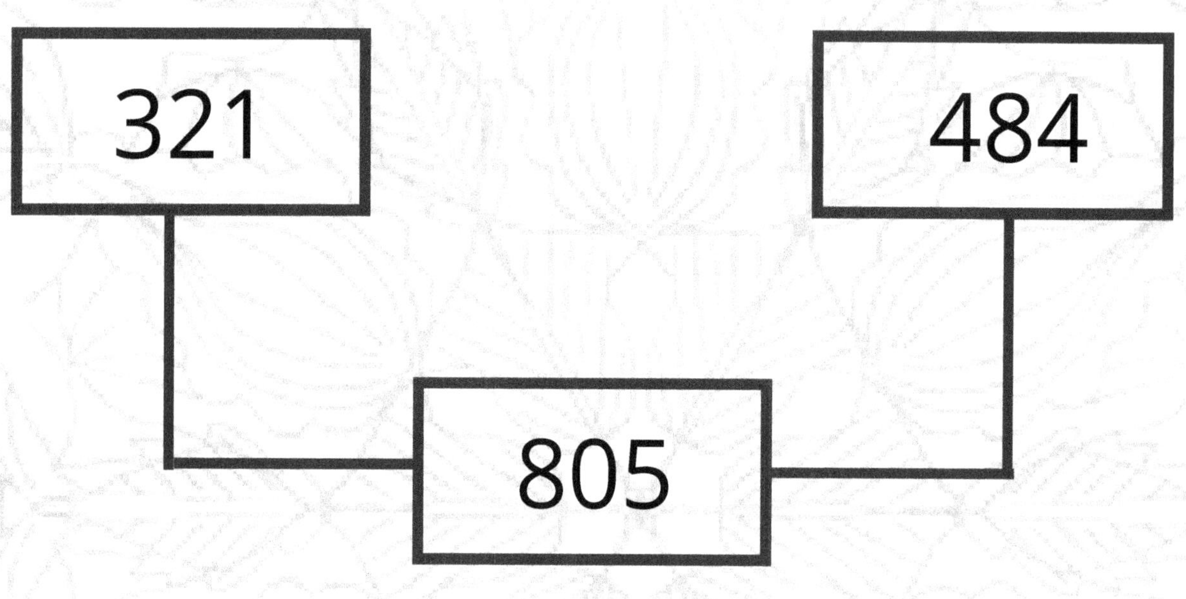

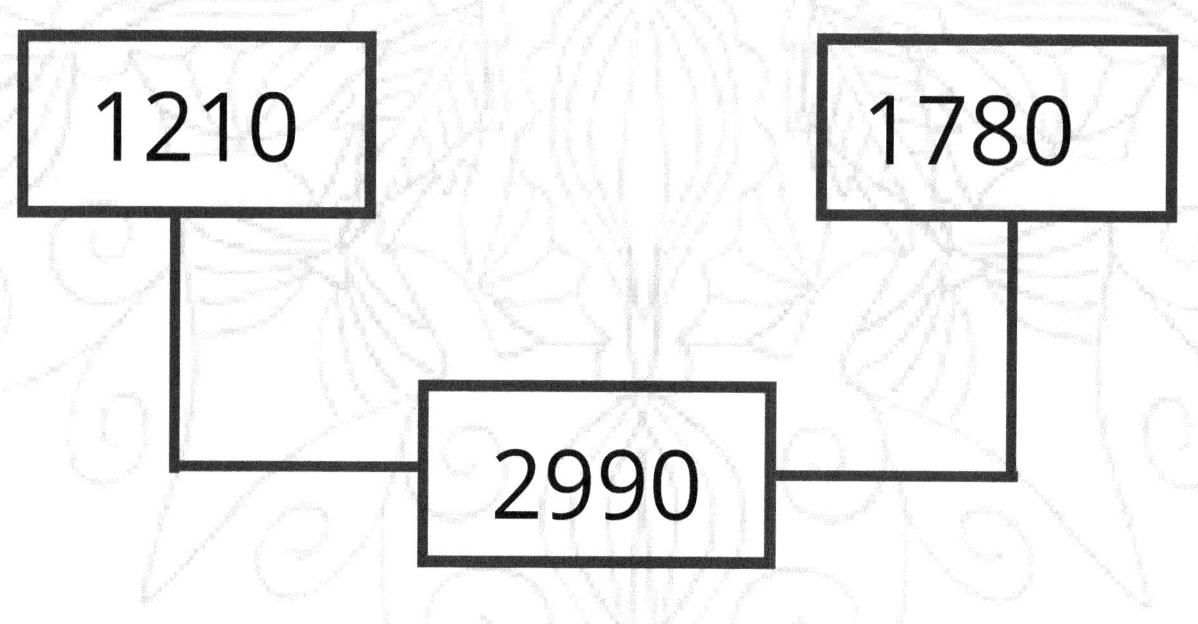

Exercise 1

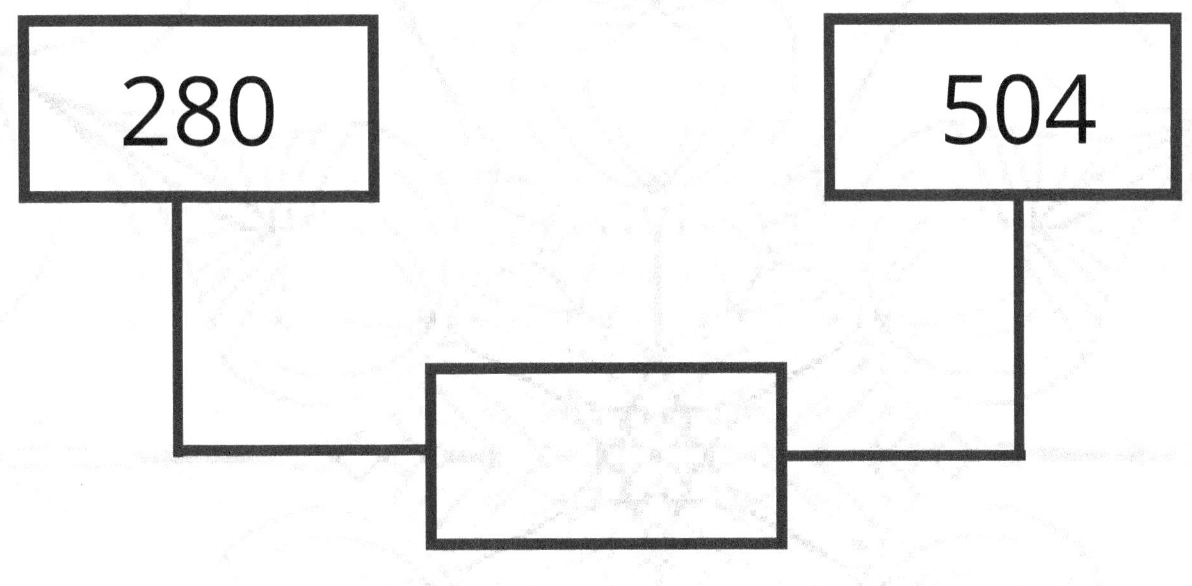

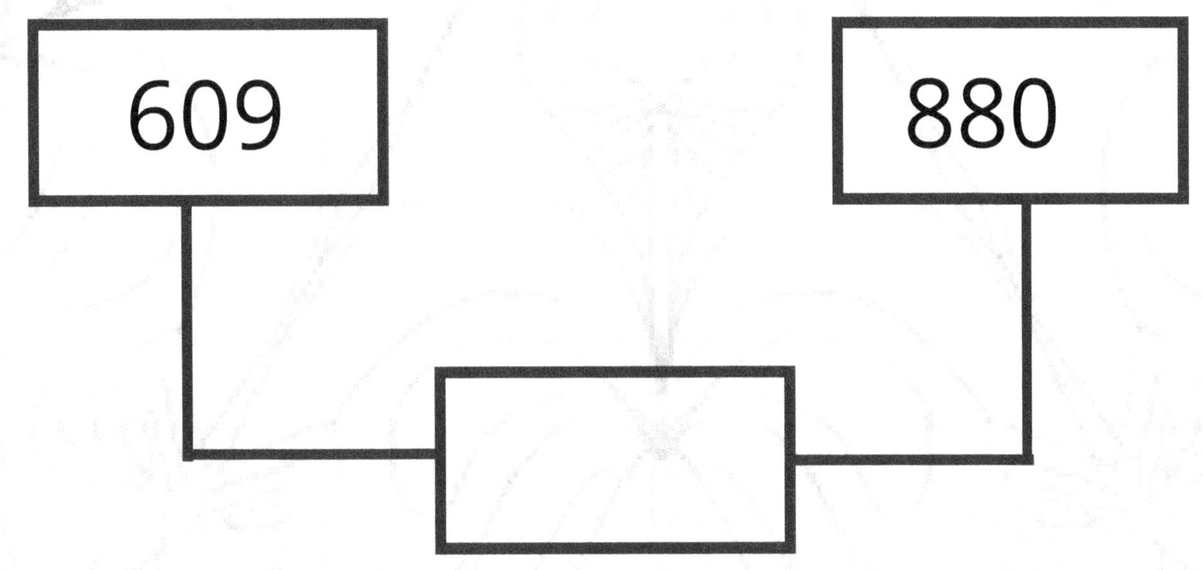

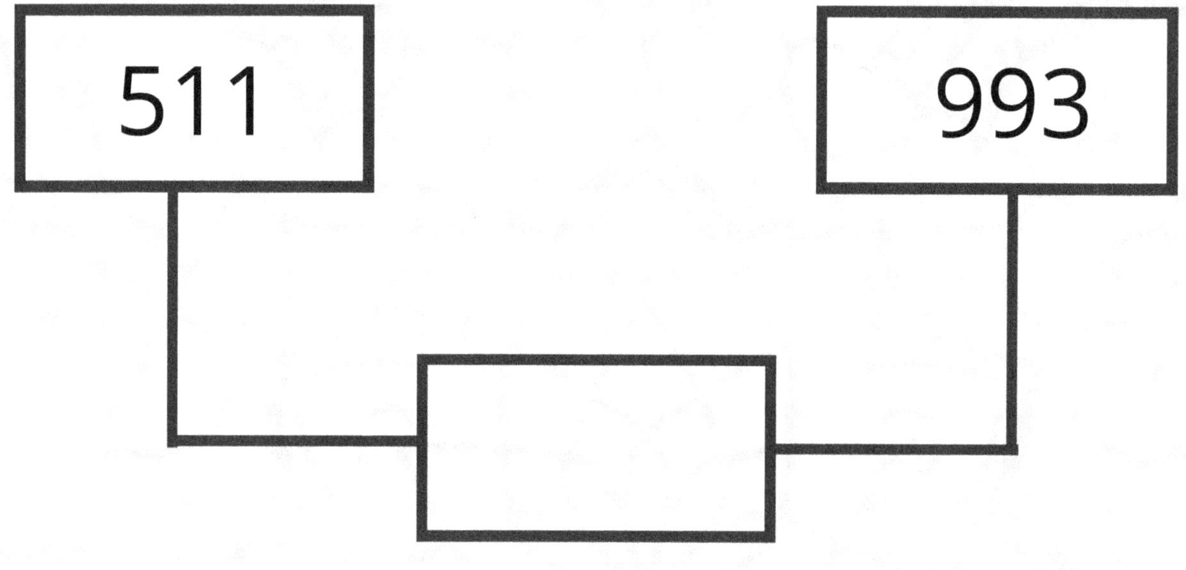

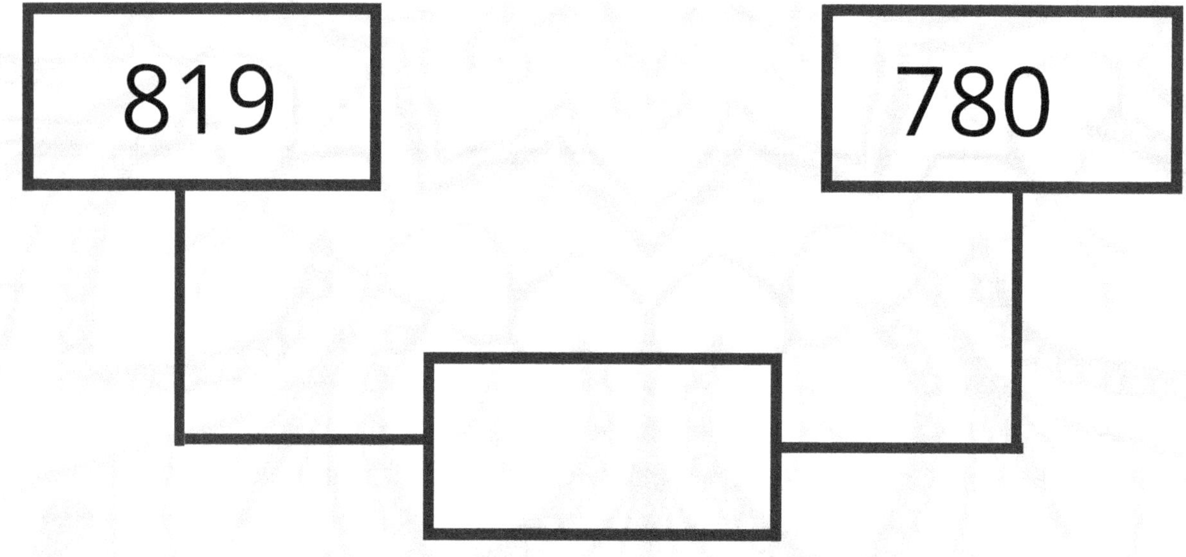

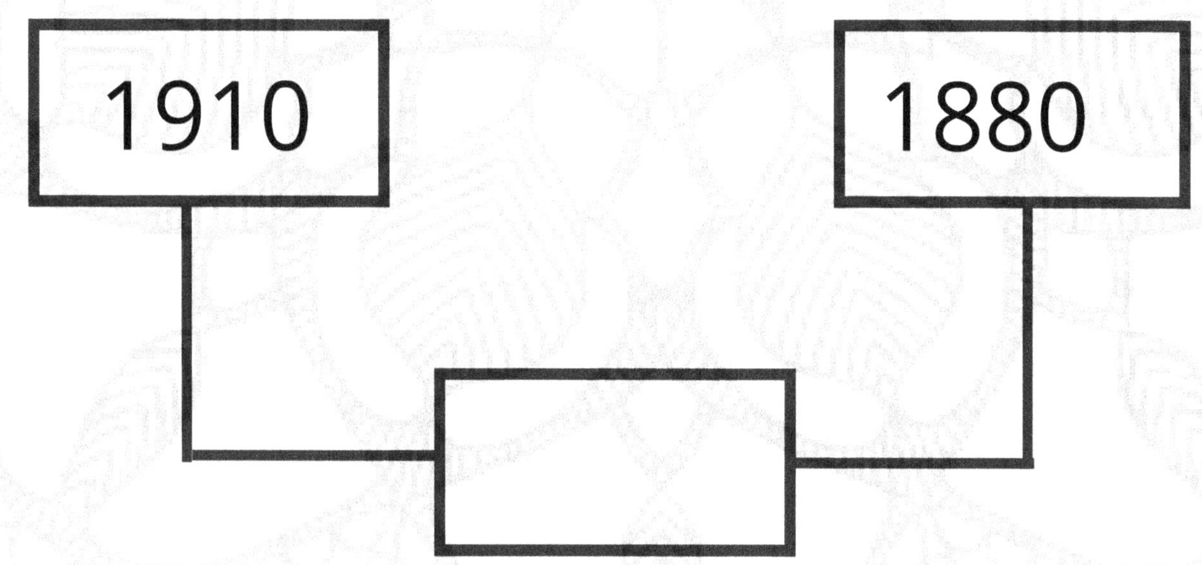

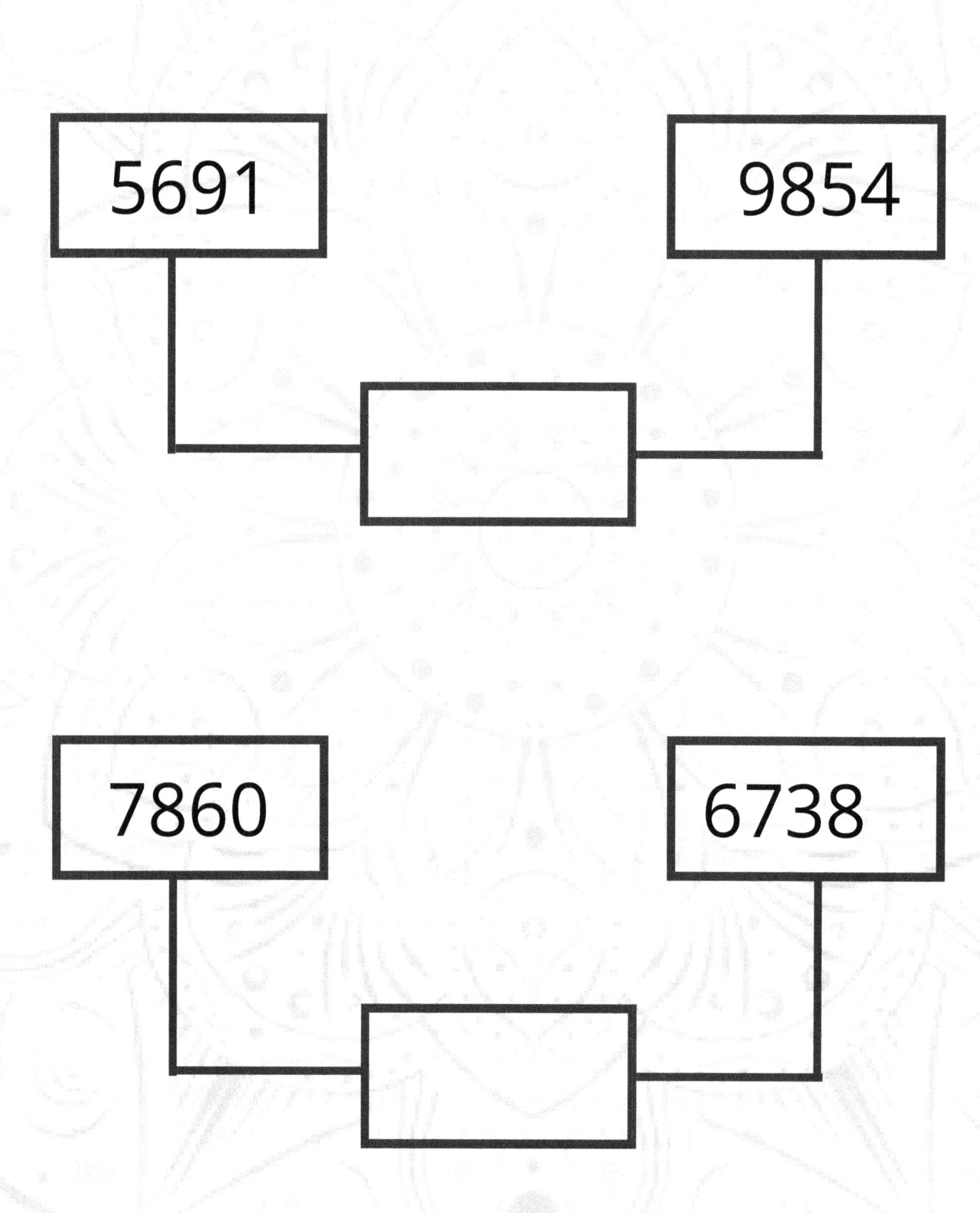

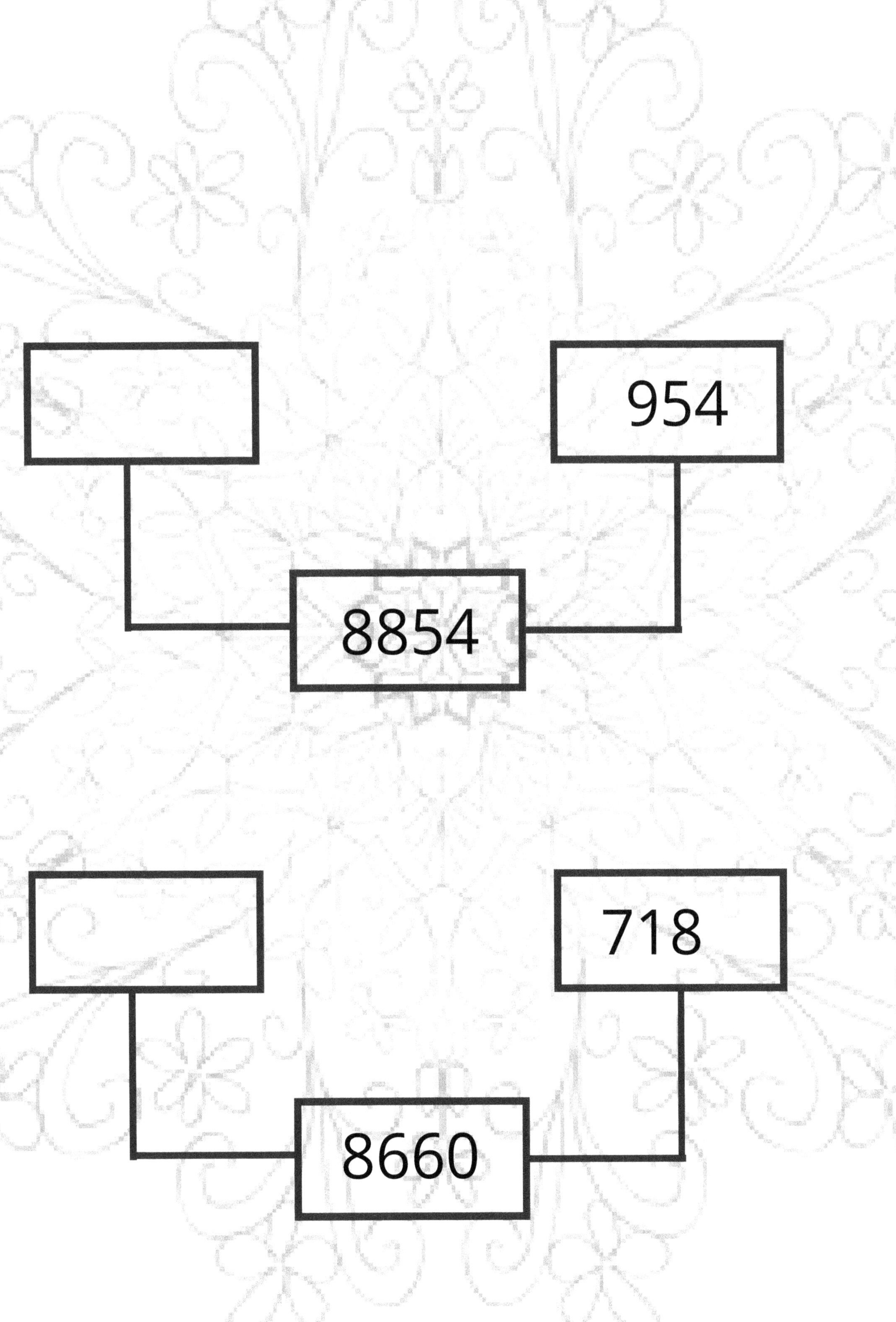
954
8854
718
8660

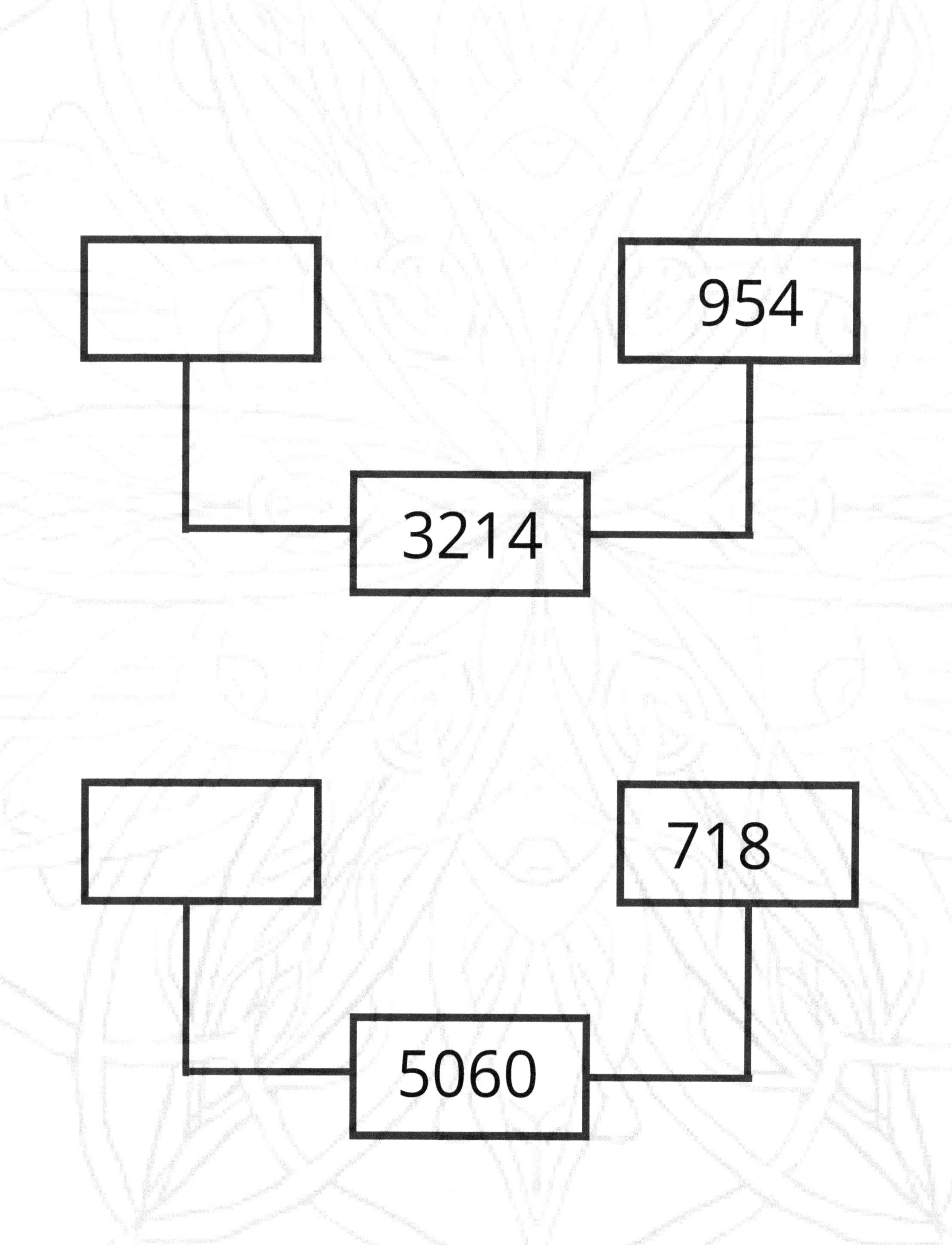

954
3214
718
5060

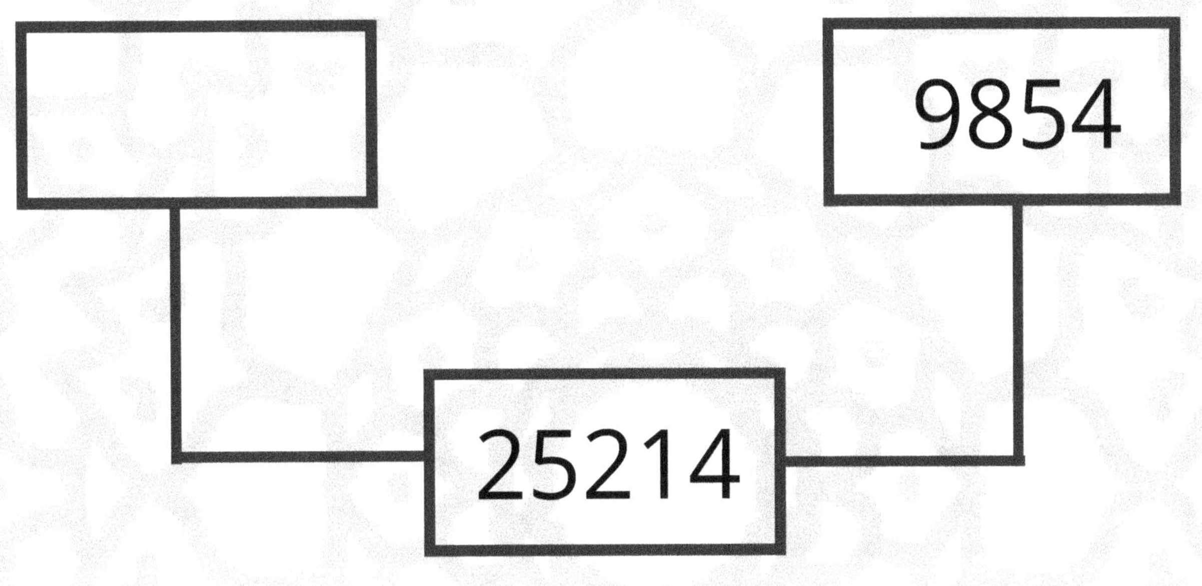

9854
25214

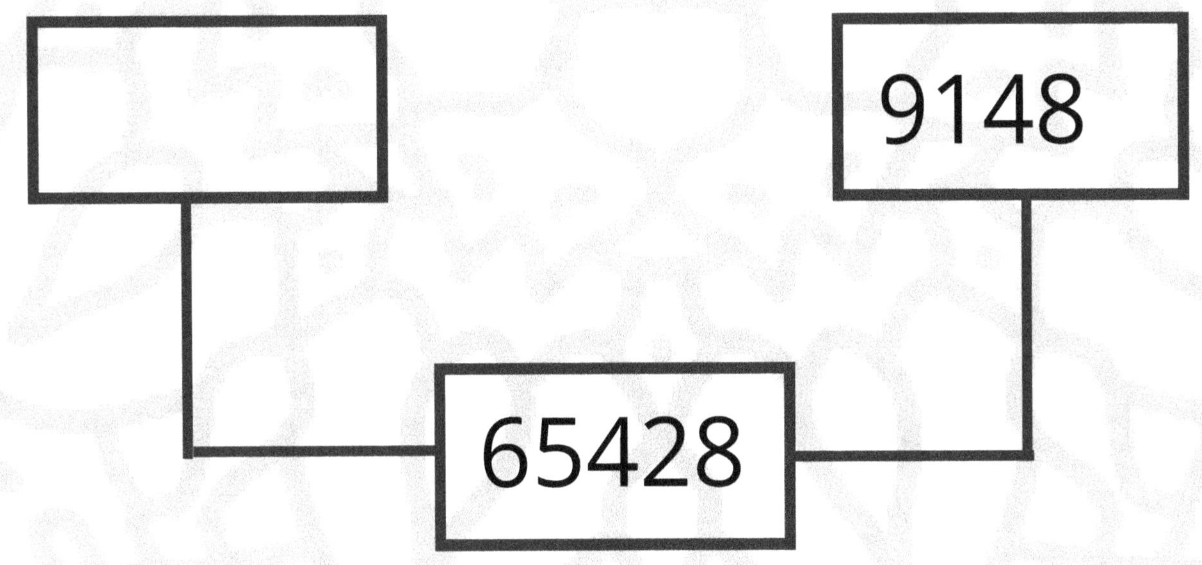

9148
65428

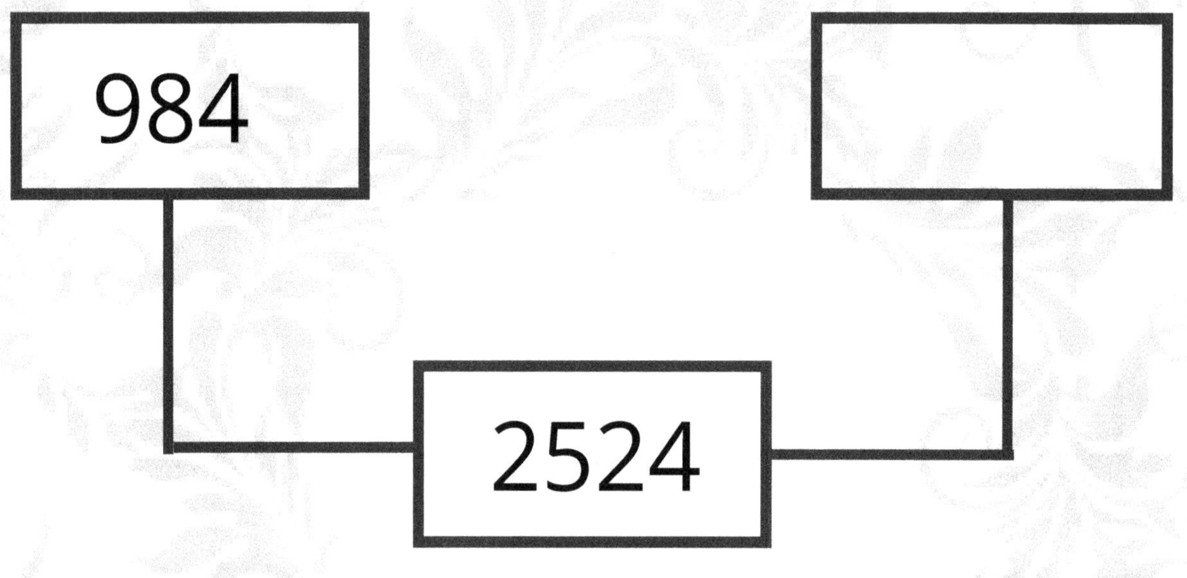

984
2524

543
5428

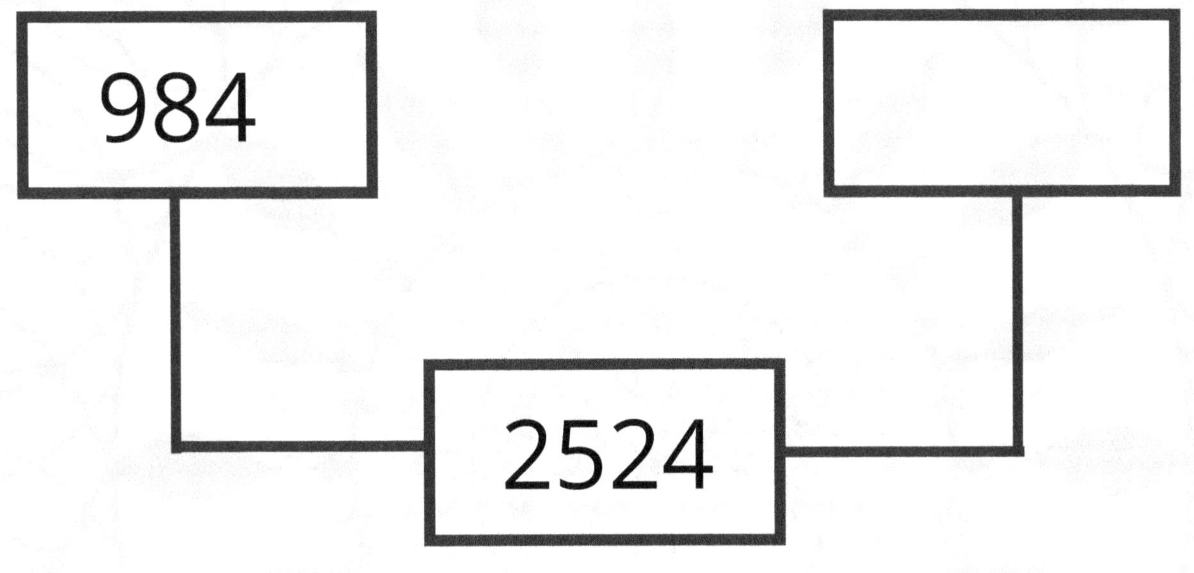

984
2524

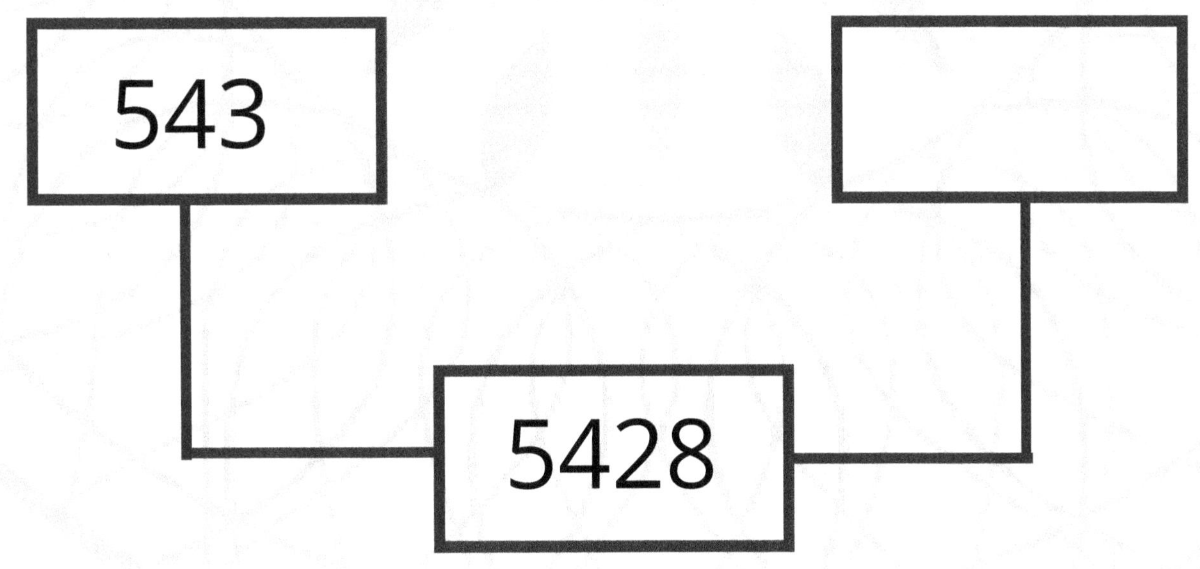

543
5428

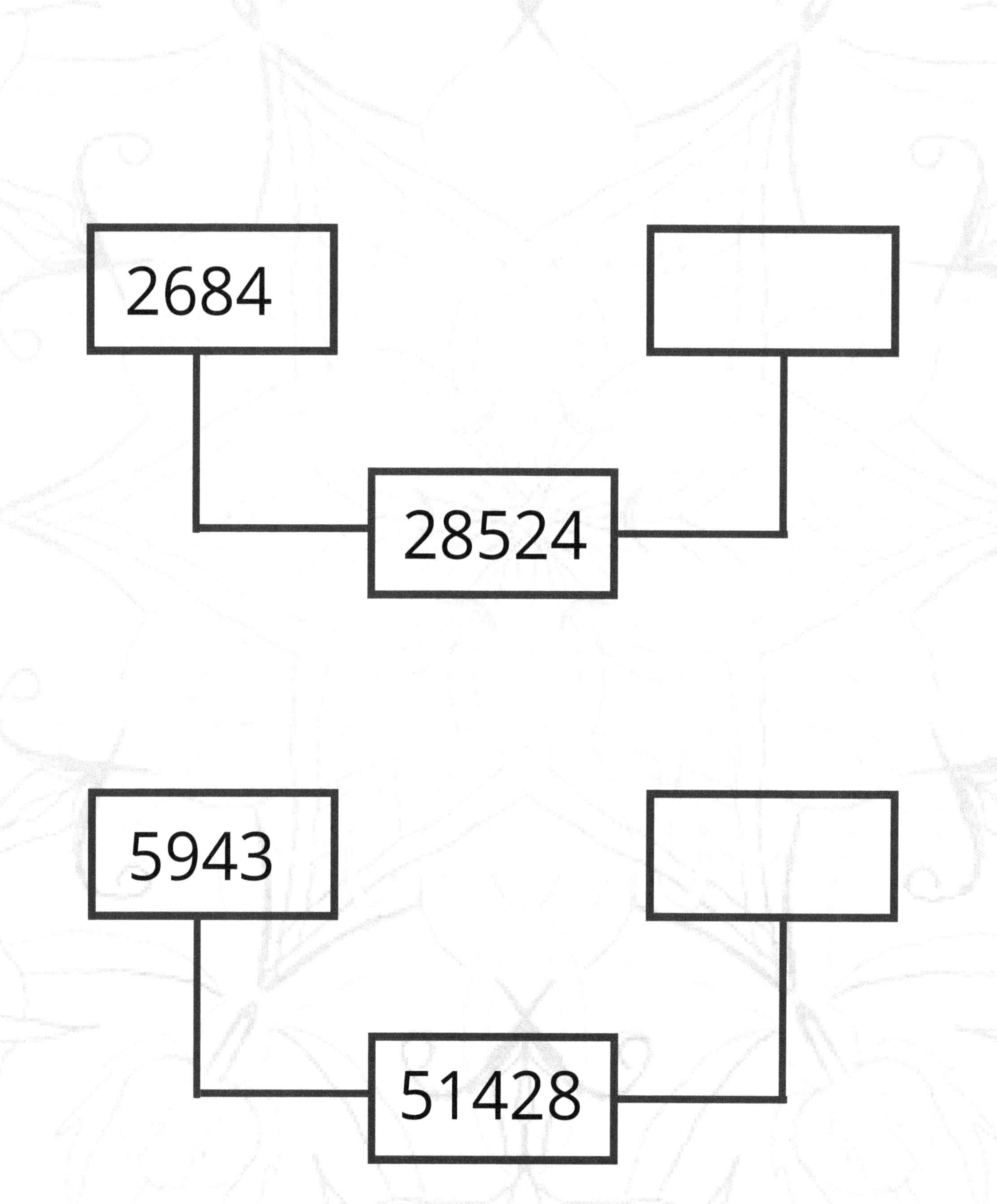

2684
28524
5943
51428

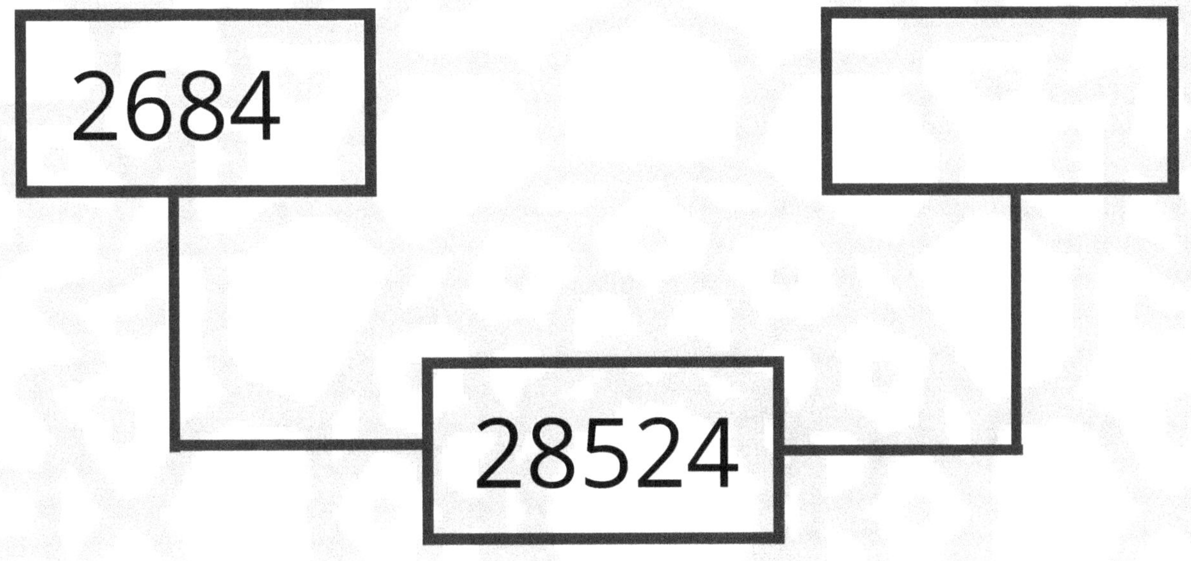

2684
28524

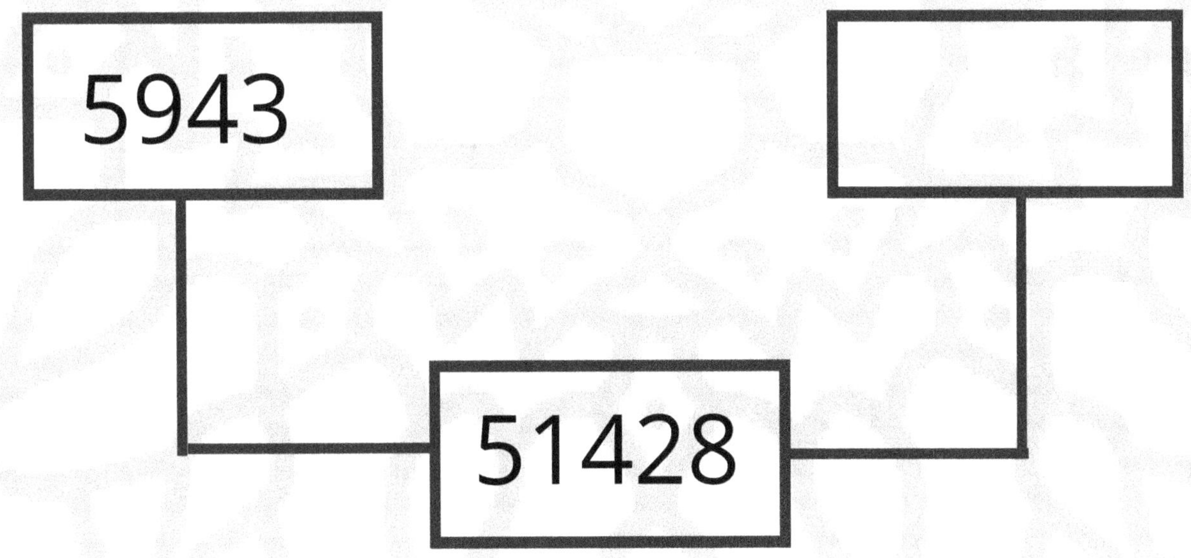

5943
51428

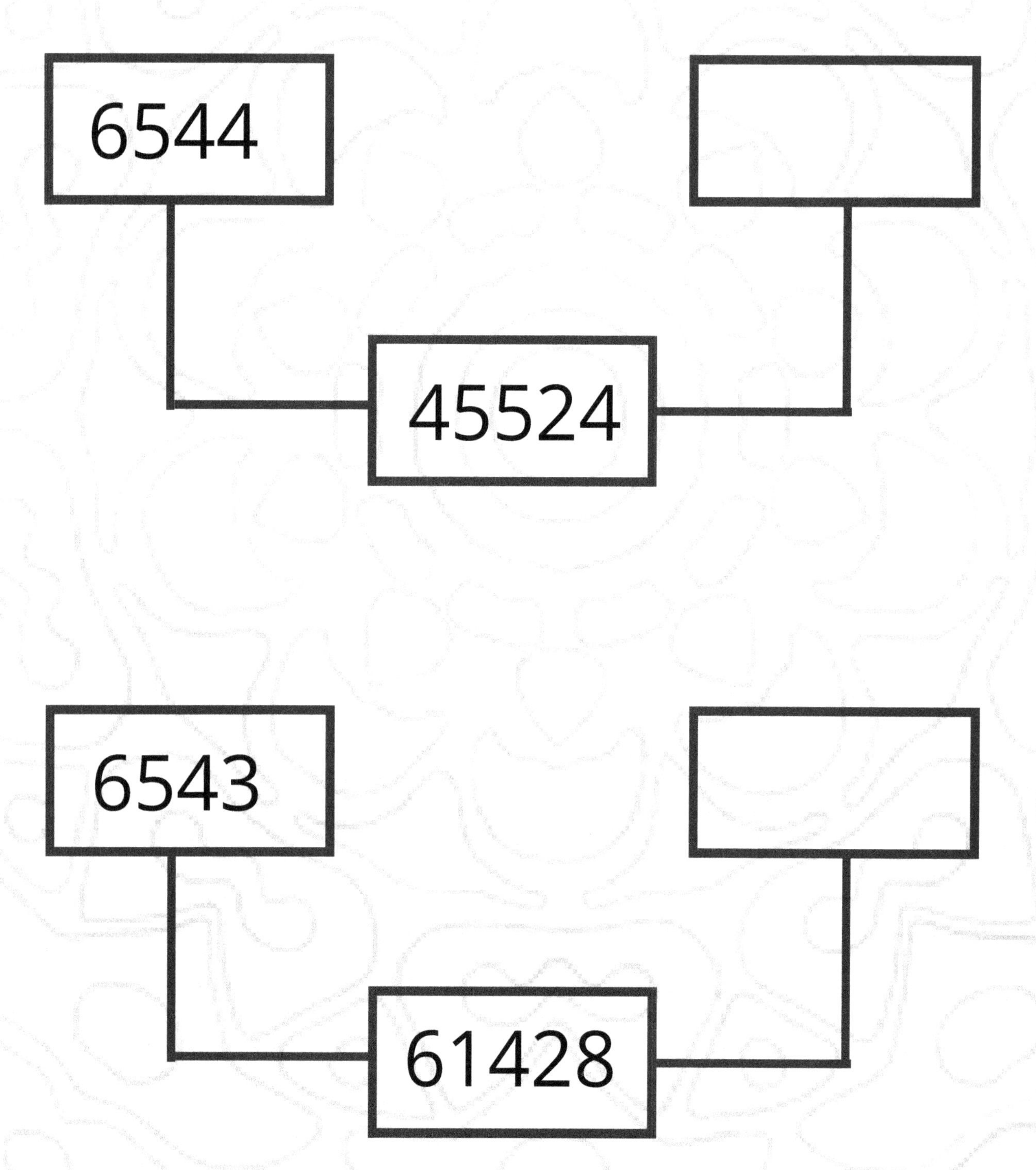

6544
45524
6543
61428

Example 2

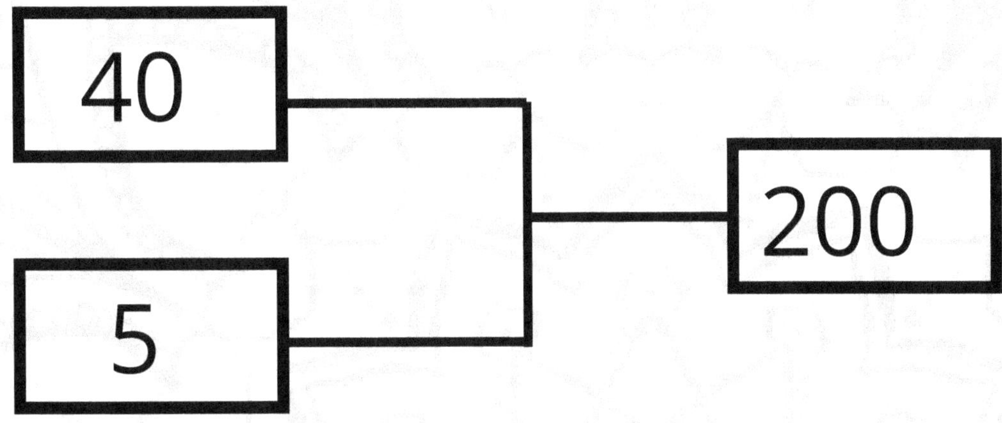

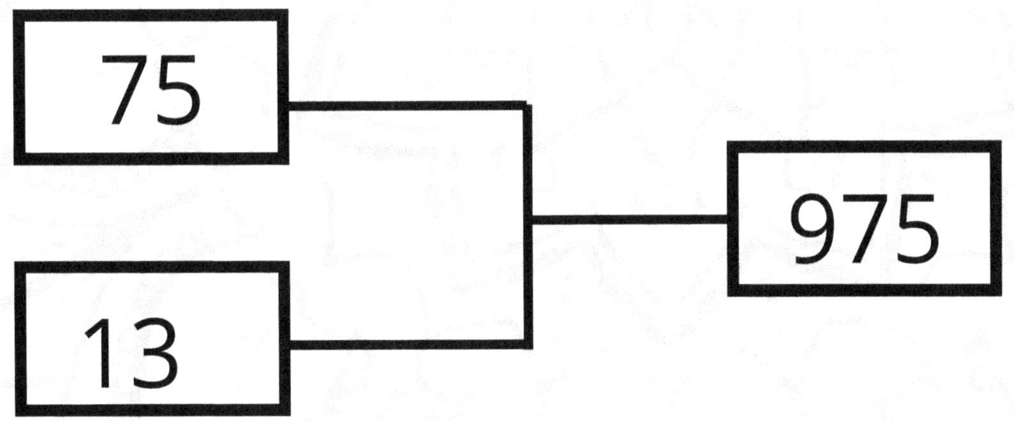

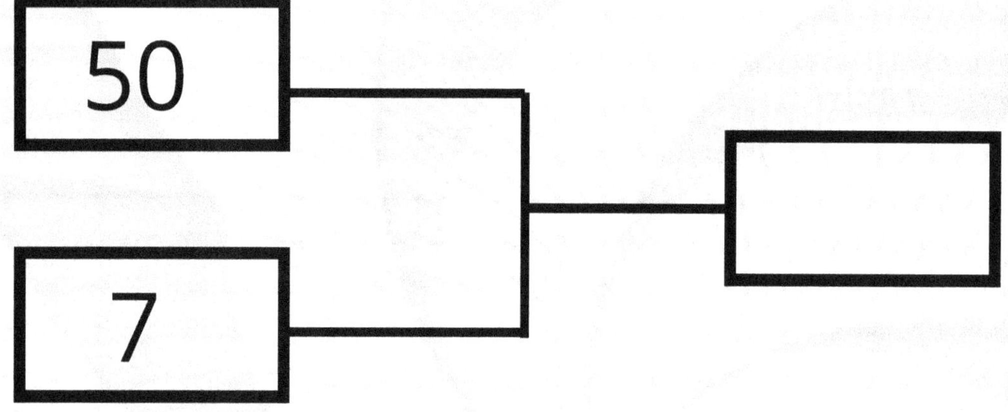
50
7

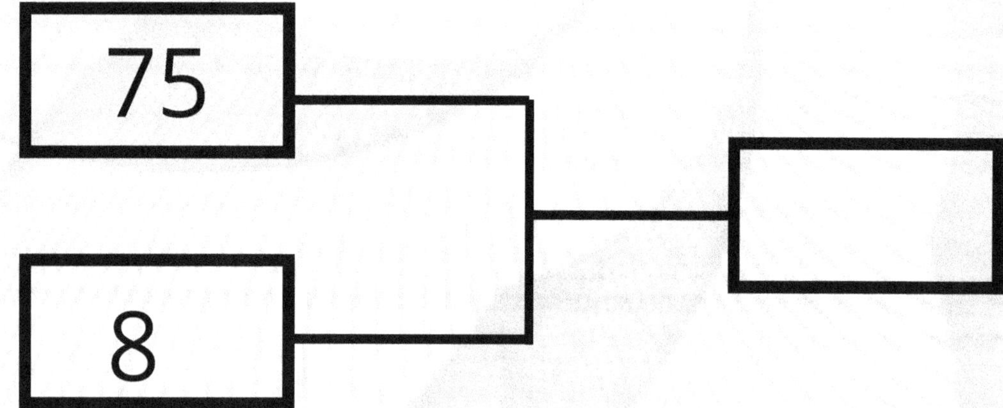
75
8

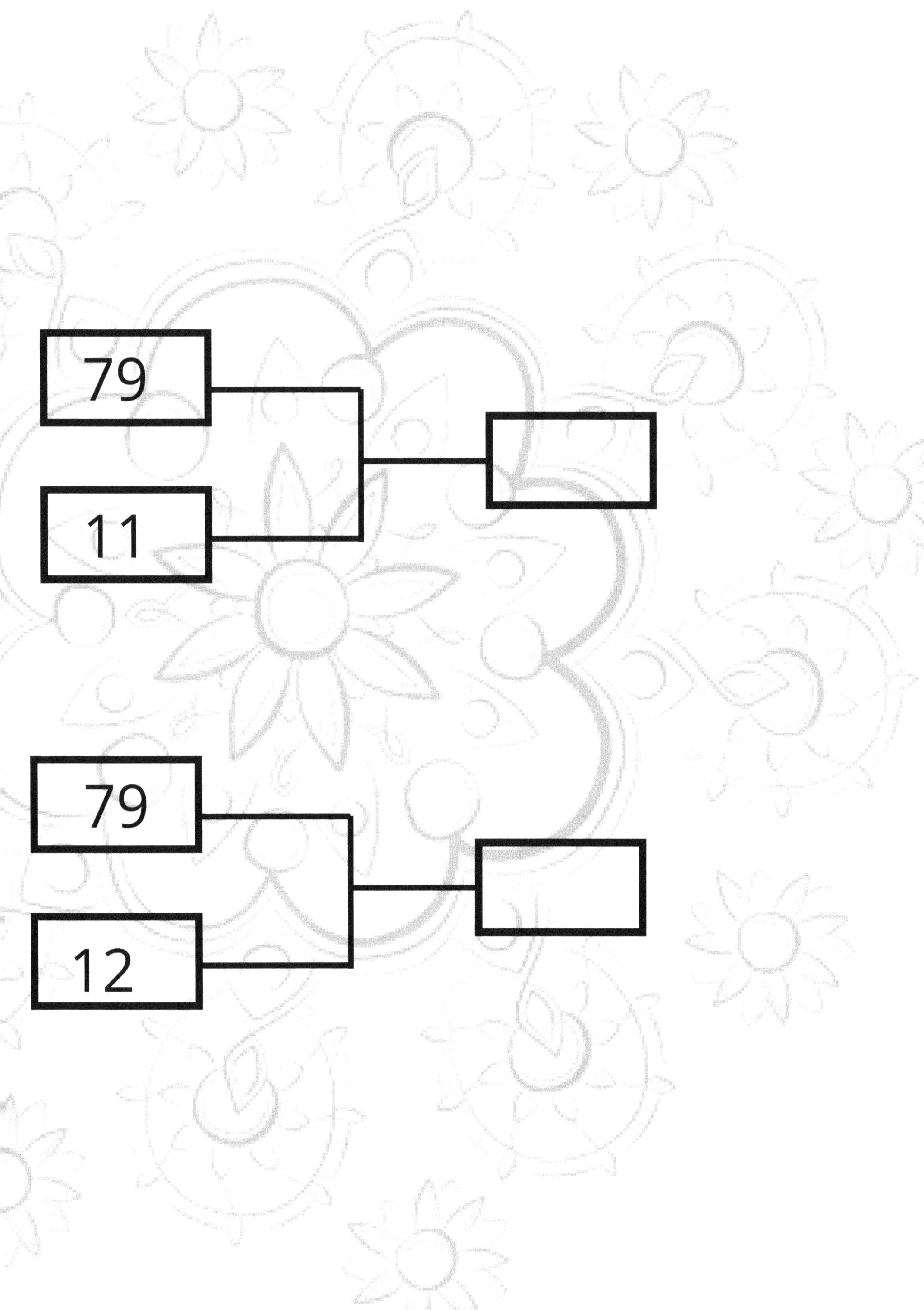

79
11
79
12

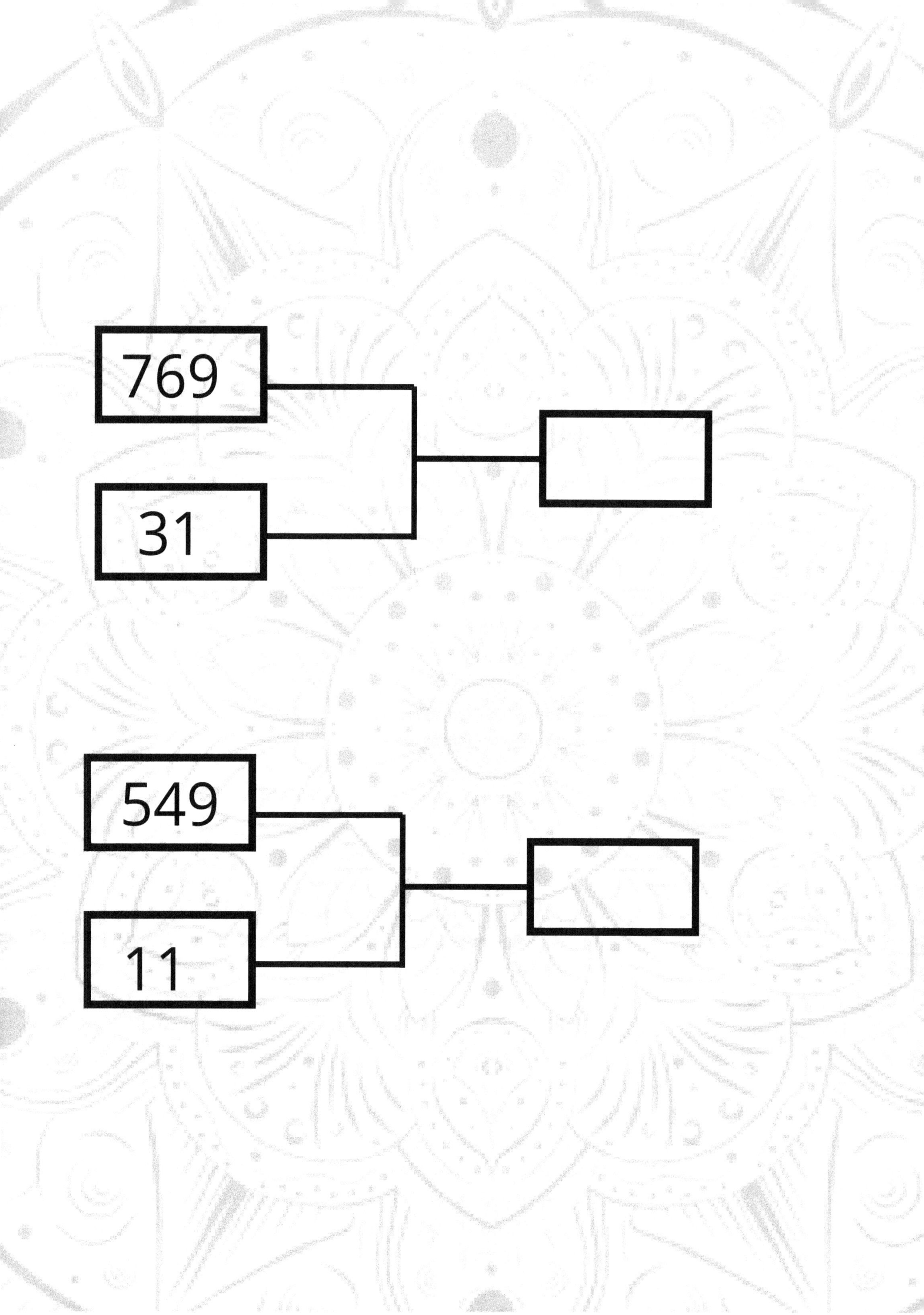

769
31
549
11

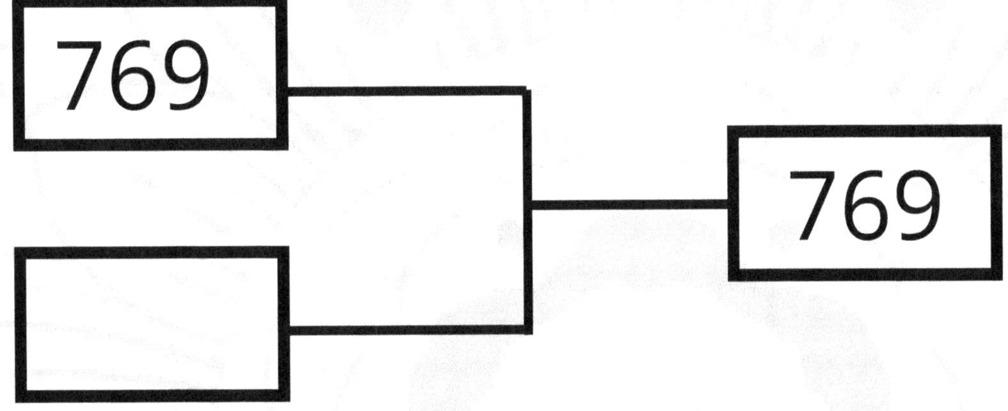

769
769

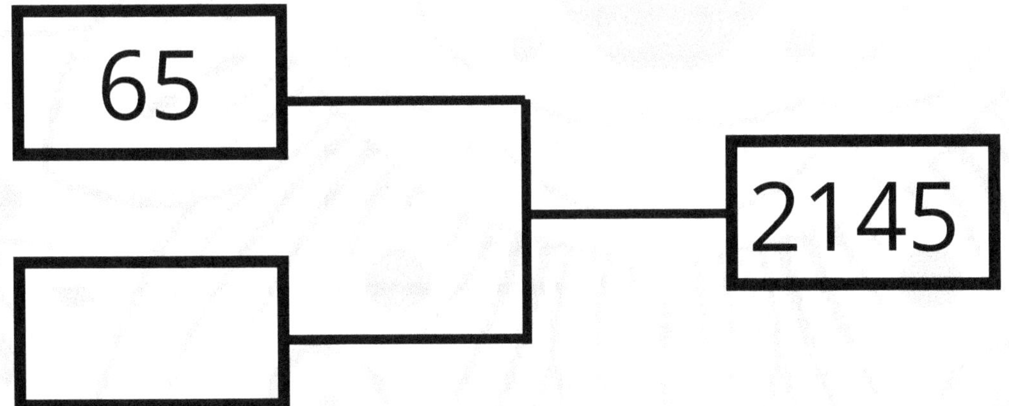

65
2145

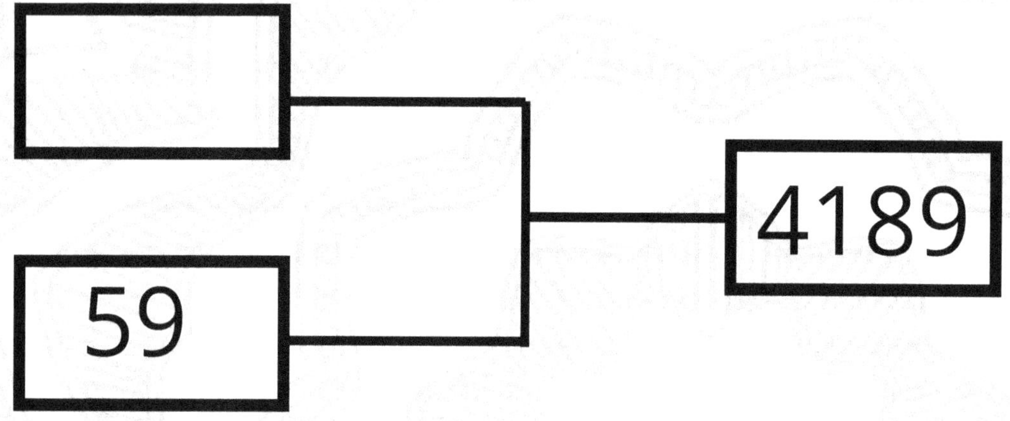

59
4189

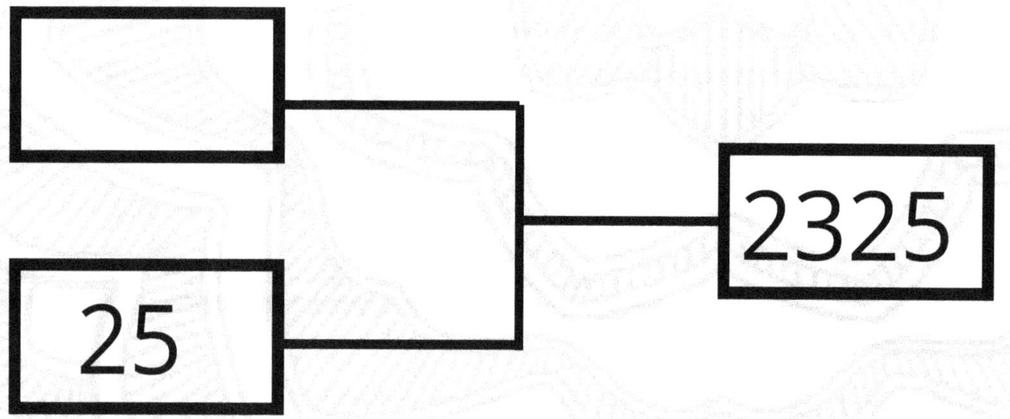

25
2325

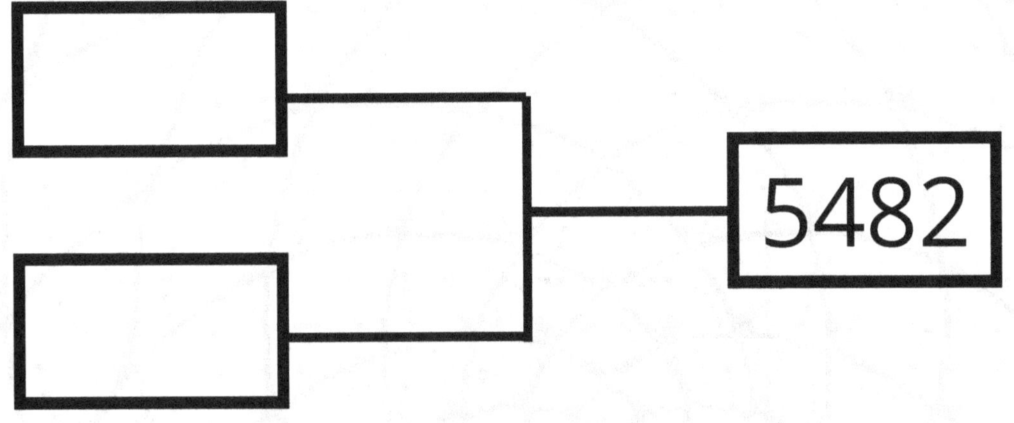

5482

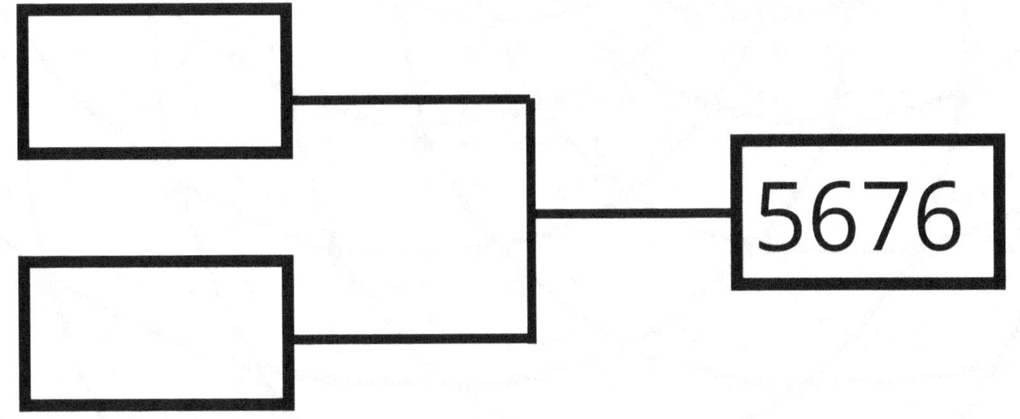

5676

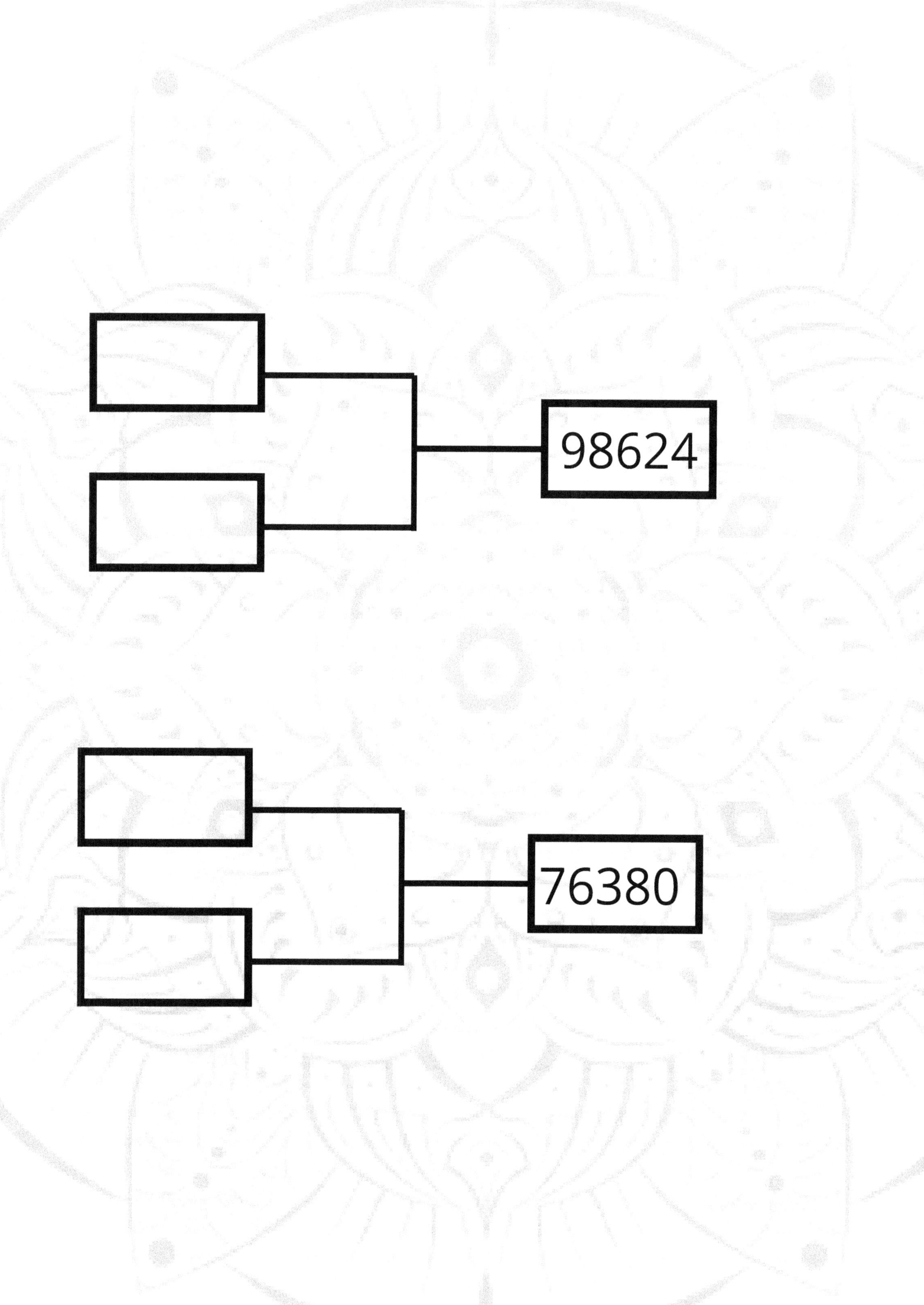

98624
76380

Example 3

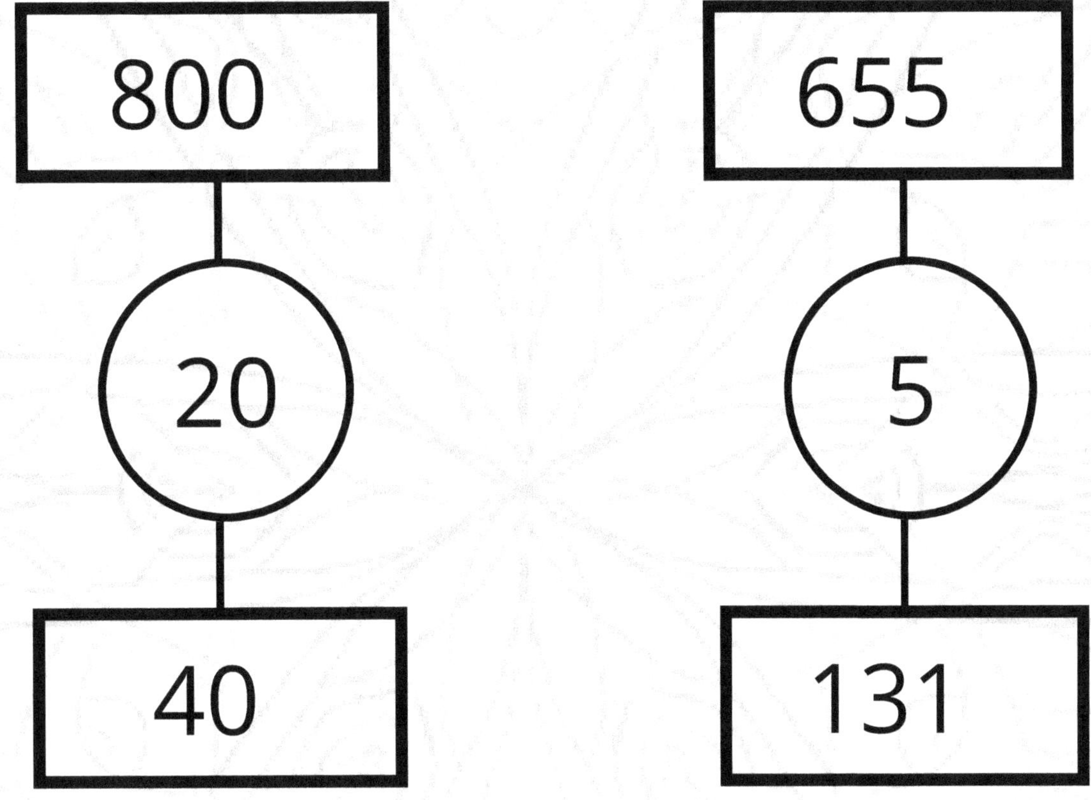

Exercise

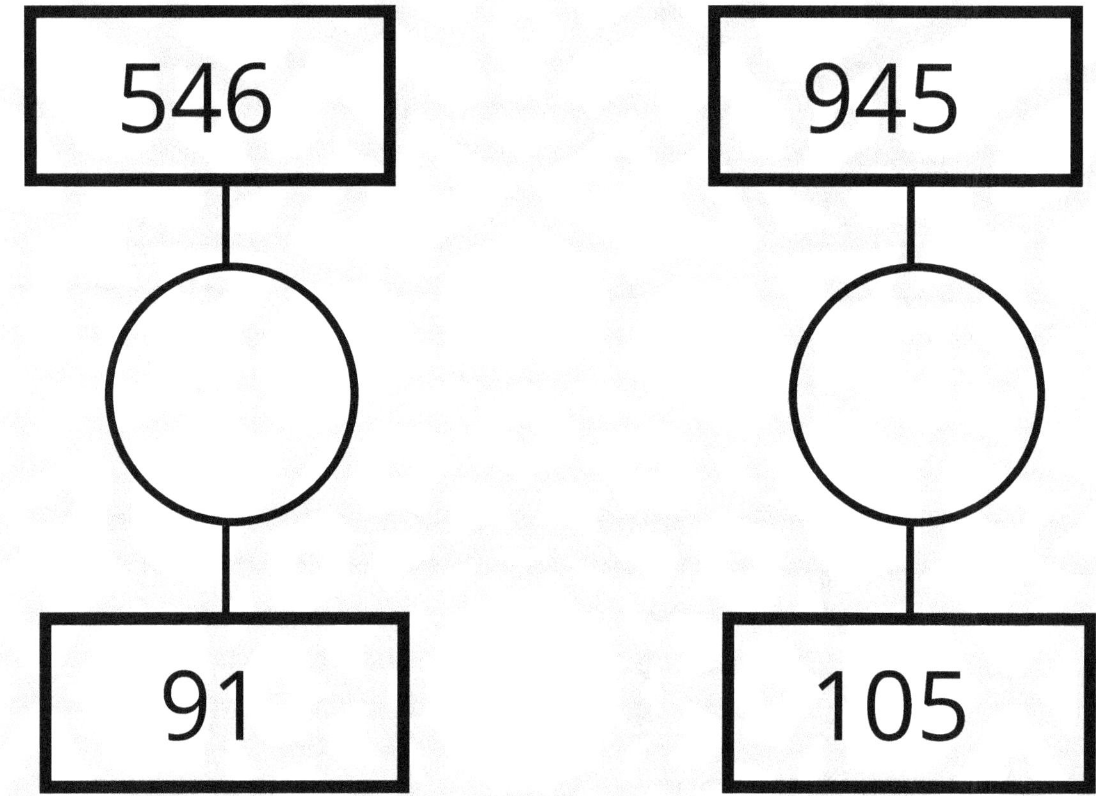

Exercise

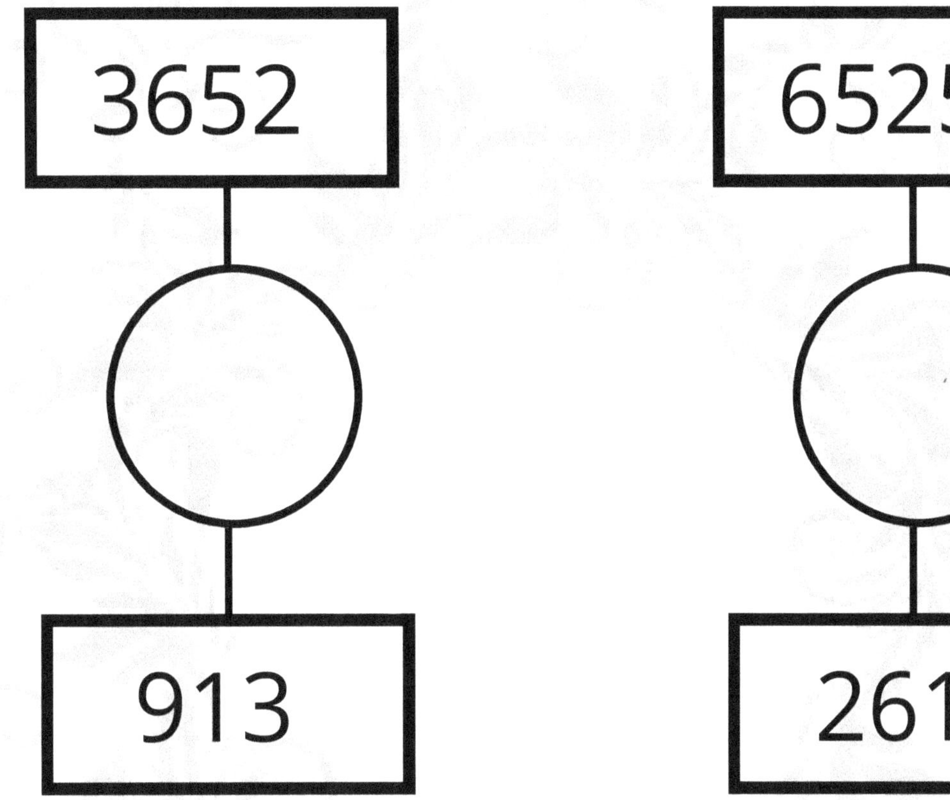

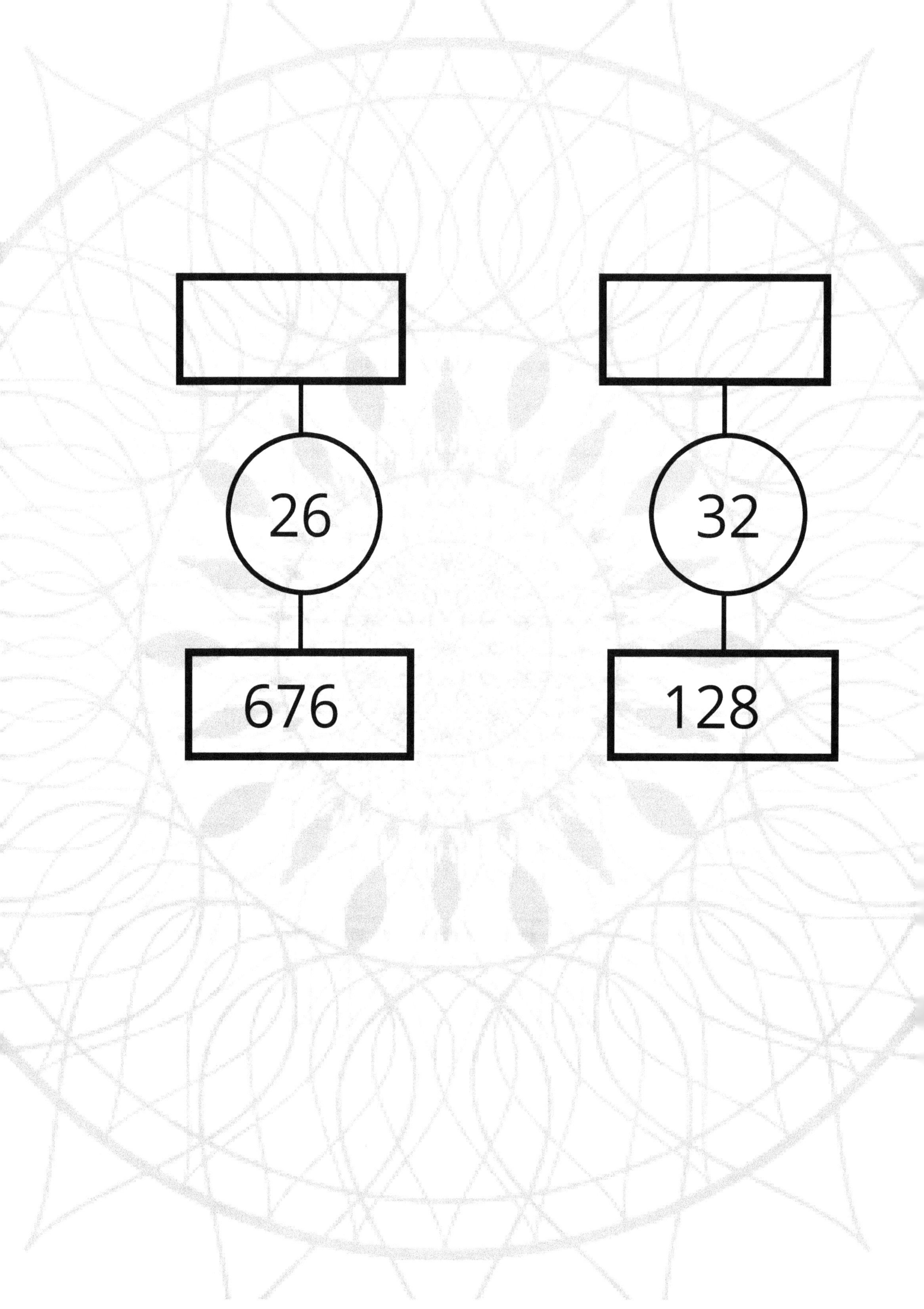

26
676
32
128

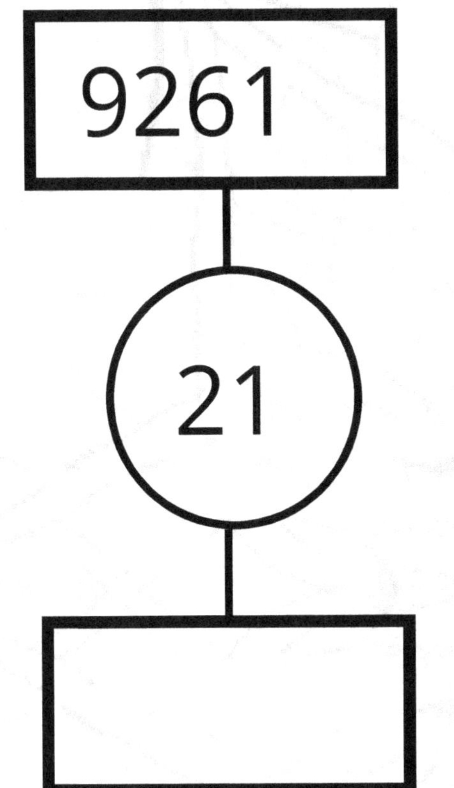

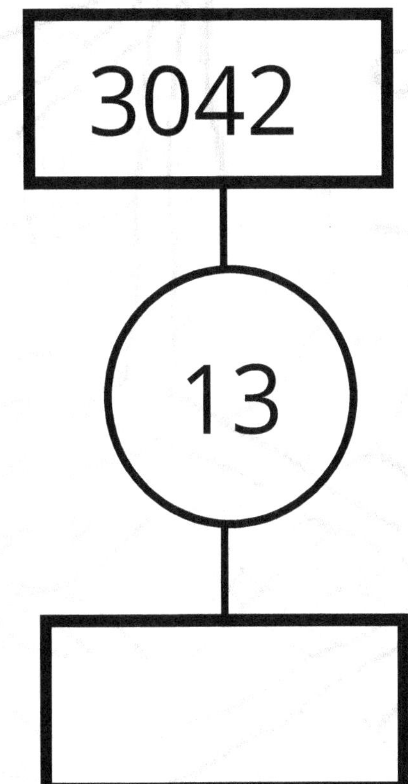

Complete the following table

+	3	4	6	2	7
1	4		7		8
4		8		6	
7			13		
5	8				
3		7		5	10

Complete the following table

−	9	7	8	12	18
4	5		4		
5		2			
3					
6	3				
2					

Complete the following table

×	9	8	10	11	13
7	63		70		
5		40			65
4	36			44	
6					
2		16			

Find the perimeter of the following shapes

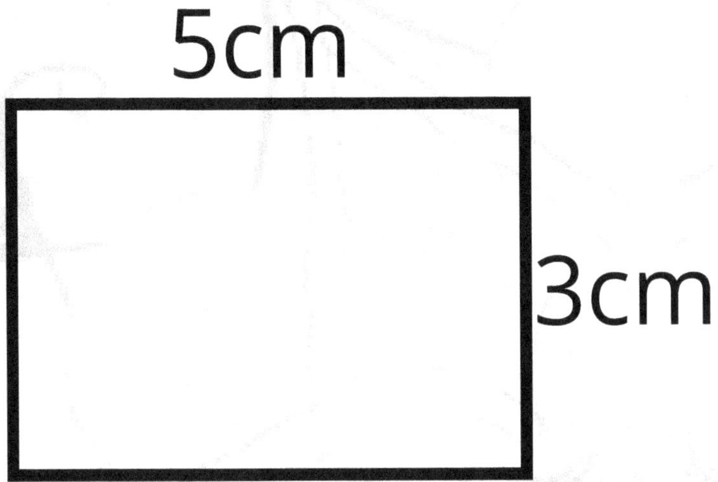

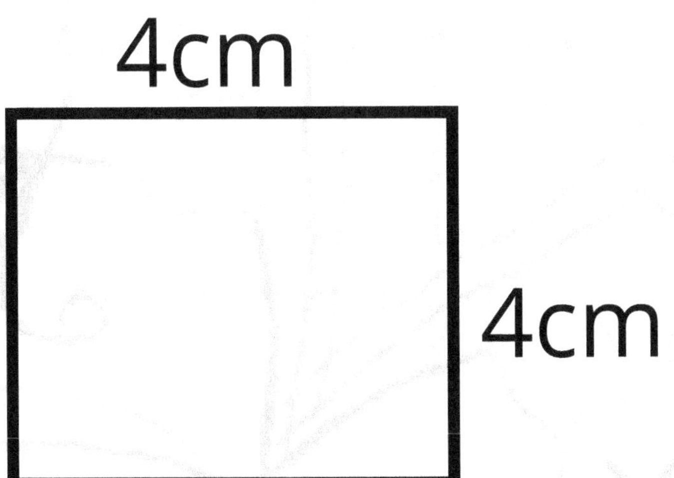

Perimeter = 2 (length + breath)

Find the perimeter of the
following shapes

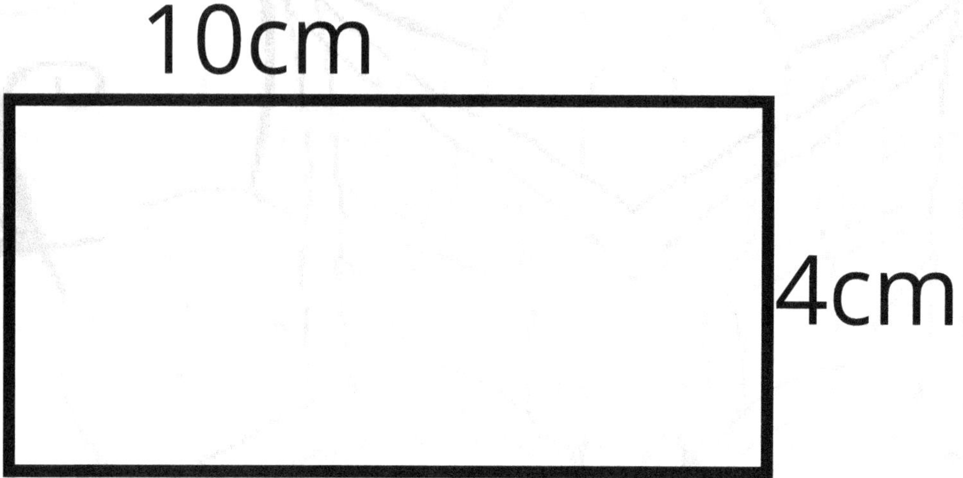

Perimeter = 2 (length + breath)